FIVE RINGS AND ONE STAR

FROM BERGEN-BELSEN TO MUNICH '72
THE STORY OF SHAUL LADANY

Andrea Schiavon

Translated by Sahar Zivan

This edition first published in 2021 by

POLARIS PUBLISHING LTD
c/o Aberdein Considine
2nd Floor, Elder House
Multrees Walk
Edinburgh
EH1 3DX

Distributed by
Birlinn Limited

www.polarispublishing.com

Text copyright © Add Editore, 2012
Translation copyright © Sahar Zivan, 2021
Acquired through Immaterial Agents

First published in Italy in 2012 by Add Editore, Torino, as *Cinque cerchi e una stella*

ISBN: 9781913538293
eBook ISBN: 9781913538309

British Library Cataloguing-in-Publication Data
A catalogue record for this book is available on request from the British Library.

Designed and typeset by Polaris Publishing, Edinburgh
Printed in Great Britain by MBM Print, East Kilbride

To Ona, Teo, Olivia, Tessa and Nina,
the future has not been written.

LONDON, MAy 12th 2022

TO

OLI & OLIVIA PARENTS,

WHO EDUCATED

SUCH NICE

"KIDS"

ABOUT THE AUTHOR

Andrea Schiavon was born in Padua and is a journalist for *Tuttosport*, responsible for covering Olympic Sports with a focus on athletics, cycling and Olympic history. He won the Bancarella Sport Award in 2013 for *Five Circles and One Star*.

ABOUT THE TRANSLATOR

Sahar Zivan is a British-Israeli translator currently living in Haifa, Israel. He holds a bachelor's degree in Italian studies from the University of Bristol and a master's degree in translation and culture from University College London. He translates from Italian and Hebrew into English, and has previously translated Claudio Fava's *The Silenced* (Polaris Publishing).

CONTENTS

ACKNOWLEDGEMENTS

The first acknowledgement has to go to Professor Shaul Ladany for sharing so many memories with me, as well as a few kilometres. In addition to our conversations, his autobiography (*King of the Road*, Gefen Publishing House, 2008) was a point of reference for fleshing out some of the details in this book.

I would also like to thank Francesca Lolli and Simonetta Luzzati from the Biblioteca Emanuele Artom in the Jewish community of Turin and my colleagues at *Tuttosport*.

Thank you to Gabriele Romagnoli for the title of chapter sixteen, taken from one of his pieces in *Navi in bottiglia*, and to Manuela Dviri for a pleasant conversation about Israel and a coffee on a late afternoon in Tel Aviv.

Thank you to: Lucilla Andreucci, Stefano Arcobelli, Damiano Beltrami, Pier Bergonzi, Luca Bianchin, Stefano, Elisabetta and Matilde Candotti Laterza, Stefano Delprete, Alessio Giovannini, Napsugar Kaposi, Tommaso Levi, Ivan Malfatto, Daniele Menarini, Jessica E. Morris, Fausto Narducci, Chiara Paesotto, Gianfranco, Chiara, Annachiara and Emma Paternicò Lombardo, Paolo and Gabriele Pellizzari, Sandra Piana, Daniele Redaelli, Margherita Morgana Sabadini, Adam Smulevich, Vanni Tosco, Giampaolo Urlando, Marco, Linda, Matteo and Elena Vallin Giacobelli, Zsolt Zagoni, Martina Zambon, Luca Zampieri and Massimo Zilio.

To my mother Lorena, Gabri, Kika, Andrea, Grandma Nina, Ona, Teo, Olivia, Tessa, Nina and Martina. In a word: family.

ONE

MUNICH, 5 SEPTEMBER 1972

A prank. Zelig Stroch enjoys playing practical jokes on his teammates. This time, Zelig is trying to convince him there is a terrorist attack under way. That is what Shaul Ladany concludes as he is awoken. Dawn is rising on Tuesday, 5 September 1972, the day that will forever change the face of the Olympic Games. Shaul's legs are stiff and aching from the 50km he put them through on the Sunday, and he is groggy from having stayed up past 3 a.m. going over newspaper articles about the race. While he was busy working with scissors and glue, adding new clippings to his scrapbook, a group of terrorists from the Black September organisation was minutes away from coming through the door to the adjacent unit. At the time, however, it was another unremarkable night in

Unit 2, Connollystraße 31, in the Munich Olympic Village. The last action before he turns off the lights is the same as ever: off come the glasses which he wears through every waking moment including during his races, the ones which give him the air of a professor, even mid-stride. The resemblance is serendipitous – Shaul does indeed hold a position at Tel Aviv University – but it confers neither privilege nor advantage in the battle for a podium finish at the Olympic Games. At the age of 36, Ladany is old for an athlete. Or young for a lecturer. A matter of perspective. Two souls sharing the same body. Tired. After the age of 30, fatigue begins to affect you in new ways – racewalking generates it in spades, but for Ladany, this is not the problem. The real weight on his shoulders is the months of training and the weeks at a time spent away from Shoshana, his wife, and their year-old daughter Danit. A few days stand between him and the closing ceremony of the Games, after which there will be more time for them.

But now he finds himself awake earlier than expected, and it quickly becomes clear that this is not a prank. At 4.30 a.m., eight Palestinian fighters broke into Units 1 and 3 and took nine hostages – among them athletes, coaches and support staff –

from the Israeli delegation. Two people have already been shot. When Shaul asks his roommates what's going on, they take him to the window and show him a bloodstain on the asphalt below. The blood belongs to Moshe Weinberg, the first victim. It all seems too much to take in. The night before, Shaul had given his alarm clock to Muni – as Weinberg was known to everyone – so that the wrestling coach could take Mark Slavin to the weigh-in ahead of his bout. Mark, who had moved to Israel from the Soviet Union four months before the Games and is still only 18 years old, is among the hostages. The other victim is the weightlifter Yossef Romano, left to die on the floor of the room where the Israeli hostages are being held.

Shaul and his roommates are unsure exactly who has been taken. Someone heard shots fired in the middle of the night and assumed it was the sound of the somewhat raucous and lively Uruguayan delegation next door. Even now that they know it's an attack, the inhabitants of Unit 2 are unaware how close the danger lies. They decide to leave via the sliding door at the back which leads to a small courtyard. 'None of us realise that, by standing out in the open, we are directly in the line of fire of anyone looking

3

out from the second-floor windows,' Shaul tells me as he remembers back to that harrowing night.

At that moment the terrorists happen to be facing in the other direction, and by crossing the grass behind the building, the group can get to safety. Once more, death brushes past Ladany, as it had in the concentration camp at Bergen-Belsen. The boy who survived the camps has become a man who escapes a terrorist atrocity, with fate determining the drowned and the saved without any discernible design.

In the meantime, the German police are already quizzing Tuvia Sokolsky and Gad Tsabari, the only inhabitants of Units 1 and 3 to make it to safety. Sokolsky escaped while the Palestinian infiltrators fought with Yossef Gutfreund, who used his 1.95 m frame and 133 kg of bulk to block the door. Tsabari managed to free himself when their assailants moved him and his five teammates from Unit 3 to Unit 1. There was a window of a few short yet decisive metres. Running in a zigzag pattern, the flyweight wrestler managed to escape to safety. Weinberg and Romano made a break for it too, but they were mown down by Kalashnikov fire. The massacre had begun.

As news of the assault begins to travel around the world, the survivors are taken to the headquarters of the Organising Committee along with the rest of the Israeli delegation. The athletes speak among themselves, piecing together what they have seen and heard, and attempt to reconstruct the chain of events. Ladany has a theory of his own and passes it on to the German police officers. 'From the way Tsabari told it, it seemed that the terrorists were trying to take the hostages away from the Olympic Village, but Gad's escape forced them to rethink their plans. I say this to one of the police officers, and then I repeat it, encouraging him to take action and search for a vehicle with potential accomplices. But he doesn't seem to think much of my hypothesis. He brushes me off, telling me he'll pass it on to his superiors.' In the meantime, Shaul is trying to understand why the terrorists chose to pass over Unit 2, crossing in front of it and moving on. There was no question of them not knowing there were Israelis inside: all the maps of the Olympic Village show that 31 Connollystraße is where the delegations from Israel, Uruguay and Hong Kong can be found. The names of the inhabitants of each unit are written by the door, and names like Weinstein do not leave much room for doubt regarding the nationality of those within. The question remains: Why spare these six athletes?

'Anyone who came into the village could consult a database with information regarding each and every athlete. The terrorists could easily have discovered that among my roommates were two shooters: perhaps the thought that their room might contain weapons and ammunition put them off.'

Dawn rises over negotiations in Connollystraße. The first deadline set by the terrorists expires at 9 a.m., while the Germans seek to buy time using any means possible. The demands for freeing the hostages are written down and thrown into the street: the lives of the nine survivors will be spared in exchange for the freedom of 234 prisoners incarcerated in Israeli jails, in addition to Andreas Baader and Ulrike Meinhof, leaders of the German Red Army Faction. Negotiating with the terrorists is Anneliese Graes, a 42-year-old police officer who put herself forward as an intermediary. In front of her is an armed group led by a German-speaking man (with a slight French accent) whose face is covered in order to conceal himself.

Black September is a newly formed organisation, but it has already introduced itself to the world through a number of attention-grabbing operations: on 28 November 1971, it claimed responsibility for the assassination of Jordanian prime minister Wasfi Tal in Cairo. Three weeks before the Munich massacre, a bomb concealed within a phonograph machine exploded in the hold of an El Al flight from Rome to Israel. There were no casualties, but Black September was ready to move to the next level.

Those who have barricaded themselves in the housing units of the Israeli delegation are no novices hoping to become martyrs: they have spent a month in a specialist military-style training camp in Libya before flying to Germany. Five of them, including the two leaders, Issa (Luttif Afif) and Tony (Yusuf Nazzal), have lived in Germany for a time, even working in the Olympic Village. These details will only emerge in the subsequent investigations. During the initial hours of negotiations, the German police are unable even to establish the precise number of terrorists, a detail which will become tragically decisive in the failed attempt to free the hostages.

'I am convinced that the Germans are planning some kind of rescue operation,' recalls Ladany. 'There's a surreal situation within the village: despite the presence of thousands of armed policemen, outside Connollystraße everything seems calm.' Many athletes carry on with their daily routine as if nothing is happening.

'I saw a dismaying thing earlier in the day during a trek through Olympic Village,' *The Washington Post* journalist Shirley Povich would later write. 'With two of their colleagues dead and 11 others in the hands of terrorists only a few blocks away . . . rock music blared from transistor radios. Not a ping-pong table was empty. Laughter was heard everywhere.' For hours afterwards, the Olympics continue as if nothing is happening, until international pressure forces the International Olympic Committee (IOC) to suspend competitions. The US swimmer Mark Spitz, winner of seven gold medals in the pool, hastily convenes a press conference. He is thought to be another potential target on account of his Jewish roots, which means there is a heavy security presence around him. Within a few hours, a decision is taken to transfer him to London.

The scene unfolding in Munich could have come from a film set: there is the circumscribed space within which the action is taking place, and all around it is the outside world, partly curious and partly pretending nothing is happening. On the one hand are snipers disguised as athletes, moving around the rooftops with their weapons. On the other are thousands of genuine athletes, barely even aware of the events taking place a few steps away. The ones who *are* aware crowd around to catch a glimpse; the others carry on with their daily routines of training and pre-race downtime. In the middle of it all, tragic and almost invisible, are the survivors. 'I try to call my wife Shoshana, to tell her that I am alive and safe, but for a long time the lines to Israel are busy. My name doesn't appear on the list of survivors sent out to the media, which means that on the evening news I'm not listed among those who managed to escape.' Midnight has passed in Germany before husband and wife are finally able to speak. At the same time, a full-scale battle is under way at the Fürstenfeldbruck Air Base. At approximately 10.20 p.m., Ladany watches helplessly as the hostages and terrorists leave the village aboard two helicopters. 'From the windows of the building we were taken to, we can see them pass in front of us, with their hands tied behind their backs. Zelig Stroch, who's a shooter, tells me that from our position he could hit a number of terrorists with his rifle.' The Germans have a different plan, however. They want to move the action away from the village, and to mount their response at Fürstenfeldbruck. And so the Israeli delegation watches, powerless to intervene, as their companions are flown away. This painful sight will later be described by Zvi Zamir – then head of the Mossad, Israel's secret services, who has been flown to Munich urgently – as 'after the Holocaust . . . Jews once again walking tied on German land'.

A few hours later, events appear to have reached a happy conclusion. At 11.31 p.m., Reuters sends out the following breaking news: *All Israeli hostages have been freed.* It is a cruel lie. The report is based on a statement delivered in front of the gates to the air base by a civilian wearing a cap that identifies him as a member of the Olympic staff. The announcement is false, but is later reinforced by the German authorities. In front of the ABC News cameras, the West German government's spokesperson, Conrad Ahlers, appears relieved: 'I am delighted to announce that the information we have at the moment is that the police operation has been successful. Naturally, this has cast an unfortunate shadow over the Olympic Games, but if everything goes as we hope . . . it will all be forgotten within a few weeks.' The headline in the *Jerusalem Post* the following morning declares: 'Hostages in Munich Released.' In Italy, the front page of the *Gazzetta dello Sport* announces: '*Salvi gli Israeliani*' – the Israelis have been saved.

Tuttosport writes: 'At the airport, the police opened fire and freed the hostages.' By the time they reach the newsstands, however, it has already become clear that the real picture is very different to the original report. The Black September attack has ended in the worst way possible: the athletes are all dead, and with them five of the eight terrorists and a German police officer. In the UK, *The Times* breaks the news with the frontpage headline: 'Israeli Olympic hostages all killed.' *The Guardian* runs with the simple, haunting headline: 'The tragedy at Munich.'

The night of 5 September leaves scars that the survivors and the families of the victims struggle to forget. Ladany and his teammates stay up to receive updates. 'At around 2 o'clock in the morning, German radio announces the release of all the hostages, and we celebrate and hug each other. Finally, we can go to sleep in peace. A few hours later, I am awoken by Zelig Stroch's sobbing, and he tells me, "They're all dead."' The new day is one of mourning, a pain that the IOC seeks to channel through cursory remarks made by the president of the International Olympic Committee, Avery Brundage, in an event held at the Olympic Stadium. In his speech, the former US athlete, whom many referred to as having 'a discus where his heart should be' (a reference to his track and field career), dedicates a grand total of 28 words to the Israeli victims: 'Every civilised person recoiled in horror at the barbarous criminal intrusion of terrorists into the peaceful Olympic precincts. We mourn our Israeli friends, victims of this brutal assault.' In front of 80,000 people, Brundage draws a parallel between the pain of the massacre that has just taken place and his own personal disappointment at the boycott of Rhodesia, which has been excluded from the Olympic Games as a consequence of its racist policies. He concludes his speech with five famous words: 'The Games must go on.'

The teammates of the murdered athletes are asked to return to Connollystraße to gather the personal effects of those who are no longer among the living. So Ladany and the others find themselves back in the rooms which still bear signs of the massacre, the bloodstains on the walls. It's a distressing task that is interrupted by sounds from outside: a male voice is in discussion with the German police officers assigned to protect the surviving Israelis. 'It's my friend Alfred Badel. He's crying, and he grabs me as soon as he sees me. He looks like he's seen a ghost. That's how I find out that many people think I died during the assault.' At first, Shaul Ladany was not listed among the survivors, and around the world people have begun to pay homage to him. At a race in Denmark, the participants are informed that candles will be lit and a minute's silence observed before the start. One newspaper laments that the Israeli racewalker 'was unable to escape his fate in Germany a second time', while the pages of the *Süddeutsche Zeitung* express sorrow 'for an interview that will never be finished'.

Yet Shaul Ladany is not only alive, but also determined to ensure his voice is heard. When he is informed of the decision to return the entire delegation to Tel Aviv, he is strongly opposed. 'Abandoning the Olympics [is] like giving another victory to the terrorists.' Shaul's opinion is not sought, but he is not shy about expressing it, and his opportunity comes a few months later when the Zionist Organization of America invites him for a series of lectures in the United States to talk about the events in Munich. 'For four weeks I toured non-stop across 20 states: newspaper, radio and TV interviews, sometimes giving up to four talks a day in four different cities. The security measures were visible and almost embarrassing: in New Orleans a police car pulled right up to the plane I was travelling on, and two agents came on board and asked where Dr Ladany was. I was made to disembark with them, among the flashing lights of the police car and the stares of the other passengers, who looked at me as if I was a criminal or a witness in some important Mafia trial.'

Ladany speaks, reminds, explains and points an accusatory finger at the failings which condemned his teammates to death. Why was there no increased security around the Israeli team, despite the known threat of attacks? Why were there only five snipers at Fürstenfeldbruck, when there were eight terrorists? Why were the marksmen not equipped with walkie-talkies, making communication impossible during the (failed) rescue attempt? Why did they not have infra-red sights to allow them to aim in the dark? These were questions the families of the victims repeated over and over again for years as part of a protracted legal battle with the German authorities. Nobody wants to accept responsibility for the massacre. For 20 years, the documents and redacted reports by the officials involved were kept hidden, but with some particularly disconcerting pages making it into the public domain. Such as the revelation that the command – located inside the aeroplane designated

14

for the escape from Germany with the hostages – was abandoned a few minutes before the operation was due to begin when the agents realised that a shoot-out within the cabin risked starting a fire. A risk to be avoided, but one that left the plan drawn up by the Germans in pieces, and meant the rescue attempt would have to be improvised. Two hours of battle ended when one of the terrorists threw a grenade into a helicopter and blew it up, the explosion and the flames killing the hostages tied up inside. The remaining hostages were raked with machine-gun fire, turning the mission into a disaster, the death toll compounded by the killing of five terrorists and one police officer.

The three surviving members of Black September (19-year-olds Mohammed Safady and Jamal Al-Gashey, and Jamal's uncle Adnan Al-Gashey) were freed from incarceration less than two months later on 29 October, in exchange for the safety of the passengers on board a hijacked Lufthansa flight from Damascus to Frankfurt. The fact that the Boeing 727 had taken off from Damascus with only the seven crew members on board remains unusual. The suspicions that this was a planned exchange to prevent additional, more violent terrorist attacks heightened when it was discovered that during its stopover in Beirut, just before the hijacking, only 13 people got on – among them the two hijackers – and all the passengers were male. Eighteen supposed hostages were worth the freedom of Safady and the two members of the Al-Gashey family, who were released from prison and taken to Tripoli via Zagreb. 'The most disgraceful part of it was seeing these images of those three terrorists receiving a hero's welcome in Libya, immediately after they are released,' says Ladany. In the meantime, however, Israel's prime minister Golda Meir had already launched Operation 'Wrath of God' – retold in the Steven Spielberg film *Munich* – that resulted in the elimination by Mossad of those responsible for the Munich massacre. It was a bloody vendetta which also claimed the lives of innocent victims, such as Ahmed Bouchiki, a Moroccan waiter murdered on the streets of Lillehammer in Norway, in front of his pregnant wife. Israeli agents had mistaken him for Ali Hassan Salameh, one of the brains behind Black September and a personal friend of Yasser Arafat.

Shaul Ladany follows all of this in the press, and, as he has become used to doing with his sporting exploits, he collects newspaper clippings about the event in a folder. A memory exercise for one who never stops looking ahead, but who has no desire to forget. Then there are the commemorations. 'Every year, if I find myself in Israel, on September 5th I go to the Kiryat Shaul cemetery in Tel Aviv, where my father is also buried.' Here, there is a memorial to David Berger, Ze'ev Friedman, Yossef Guttfreund, Eliezer Halfin, Yossef Romano, Amitzur Shapira, Mark Slavin, Kehat Shorr, Andre Spitzer, Yakov Springer and Moshe Weinberg. Eleven names held fast in the memories of the survivors.

TWO

FIFTH BIRTHDAY,
THE FIRST BOMBARDMENTS

Shaul plays with his nanny in German, babbles to his parents in Hungarian, and explores Belgrade, his city of birth, in Serbian. His is a multilingual and privileged early childhood, growing up in the latter part of the 1930s, the son of Dionys Ladany and Sofia Kassovitz. His father is a chemical engineer who settled in Belgrade after graduating from university in Germany and opened a production facility for sodium silicate and a legal office specialising in patent law. His mother Sofia's wealthy family comes from Novi Sad, in the province of Vojvodina, where Grandpa Max is the founder (and a senior partner) of the most important bank in the city.

A Skoda in the garage, full-time staff to tend to the house, itself constructed a short distance away from the royal palace: the Ladany family, Jews of Hungarian origin, are members of the bourgeois upper-middle class, and their children grow up surrounded by affection and toys. Shaul has a sister, Shoshana, two-and-a-half years older than him. He's the little one, and the first son. 'I was up to my neck in toys, and I used to drive my mother mad, exchanging them with the neighbours' children for pieces of coloured porcelain or glass.' The first cracks begin to appear in their perfect world towards the end of 1940, when Dionys Ladany is called up to the Yugoslavian military as an officer in the reserves. The war has already begun, and even a 5-year-old boy can sense it when his father stops coming home from the office every evening. This time, his father is not away on a business trip: he's at the front, first in Montenegro, then battling the Italian troops in Albania.

Despite everything, life goes on within the family. Spring has arrived, a sign that Shaul's fifth birthday is around the corner. The festivities are brought forward to coincide with a visit by his great-uncle Eugen, known by all as 'Uncle Yani'. The date is 1 April 1941, and the adults have gathered to discuss the latest, increasingly dramatic, international developments. A few days earlier, the Kingdom of Yugoslavia had been pressured into siding with the Axis Powers, signing up to the Tripartite Pact which brought together Germany, Italy and Japan. A British-backed coup d'état appears to lessen Belgrade's support for the Nazis and their allies. The situation in the Balkans is becoming increasingly complicated and perilous, especially for the Jews. While Shaul examines and experiments with the mechanical toy Yani has brought him for his birthday – a petrol station complete with little toy cars – his great-uncle attempts to convince the other family members to follow him and expatriate. The decision is not an easy one, and it means abandoning everything: Eugen Ladany had founded Kaštel in 1921, and it had quickly grown into the most important pharmaceutical industry in the country. And it's not only the family's assets that are at stake. Dionys is still at the front: leaving is unthinkable, as it would mean abandoning him. Yani is able to escape – travelling through Italy, he makes his way to Brazil. Kaštel continues to operate throughout the years that follow and is subsumed under the Pliva Institute, being first nationalised and then privatised. In 2006, Pliva receives almost $3 billion when it is sold to Barr Pharmaceutical. Fleeing means abandoning almost everything, but Eugen Ladany's decision to leave saves his life because, on 6 April 1941, Belgrade is subjected to a bombing campaign that lasts for days. Codenamed Operation Retribution, Luftwaffe pilots drop thousands of bombs all over the capital: the result is devastation. The city is almost razed to the ground, and the targets, chosen to pave the way for the Nazi invasion, are not only military. The Nazi mission is to sow destruction and terror. Among the buildings destroyed is the national library, which contains 300,000 volumes and medieval manuscripts. The body count is even more tragic: the victims are said to number over 10,000, but some estimates put that figure at more than twice that. A criminal act of aggression carried out without Germany formally declaring war. It is a massacre for which Luftwaffe commander Alexander Löhr will later be held accountable; sentenced to death and executed by firing squad in Belgrade in 1947.

When the assault begins, the explosions can be felt in the Ladany home, situated close to the royal palace. During a lull in the bombings, the neighbours arrive at the door and ask to take refuge in the basement, believing it to be safer. Trude – his mother's cousin, whose husband has been called up to the army – shows up soon after. Family and guests split up into two groups: some squeeze into the laundry room with the servants, the rest find space in the cellar, which is the next room along. 'Then the quiet is broken by another wave of bombings. At one point the entire building shakes and the noise becomes unbearable. My grandmother grabs me, throws me to the ground and covers me with her body to protect me. The heavy door of the laundry room is torn off its hinges by the shockwave and lands on her. We're covered by a fine layer of dust, and all around us people are screaming and crying. None of the occupants of the laundry room is seriously injured, but on the other side of the wall the situation is desperate: the bomb that struck the house has exploded, killing two people and seriously injuring the others.' The bombing continues incessantly and there is nothing to do but hope it ends.

A momentary window of quiet presents a chance: Shaul's grandfather attempts to start the car to no avail, while his mother runs upstairs to gather money and jewellery. The five women and two children, led by a 65-year-old man, leave the house in search of a new place of refuge, somewhere safer than a building already reduced to rubble. 'On the other side of a field we reach the house of Djiga Berger, a doctor and childhood friend of my father. We hide in the cellar of his house, along with other families who are already there, and we stay there until nightfall while the bombs continue to fall over the city.' Taking advantage of the darkness and a break in the bombardment, the Ladanys decide to leave Belgrade. Staying in the city is too dangerous – better to seek shelter elsewhere. 'We join other groups of people who, like us, have decided to head towards the mountains. When we cross a column of soldiers, a few of them yell at my mother to cover up the white pullover she's wearing, to avoid being seen by German eyes.' The march goes on through the night, all the way to the village of Sremčica, around 30km from the capital.

'There, for a crazy sum of money, a couple allow eight of us to stay in the stable on their farm and provide us with food.' In Belgrade, meanwhile, the bombs continue to rain down on the city. Shaul and his family remain holed up in Sremčica for five days. Then, when the fighting seems to have eased, his mother sends the non-Jewish maid into the city to assess whether the situation is now safer. Two days later, she returns and describes the scene: the streets are full of German soldiers, Yugoslavia has fallen to the Nazis. Nonetheless, the family takes the decision to return to the city, as it is the only way to reunite with Dionys – Shaul's father – even though nobody knows if he has survived. Their home destroyed, Shaul and the family relocate to his father's offices, and there they hide away, as the Germans have already started the campaign of persecution against the Jews, threatening to execute any who do not present themselves before them immediately. The extermination has begun, and it proceeds unabated: approximately 30,000 Jews lived in Serbia before the Second World War (10,000 in Belgrade alone), yet by the summer of 1942 – just over a year after the start of Nazi occupation – the country is officially declared *Judenfrei*: clean of Jews.

In the meantime, Dionys Ladany is attempting to return home. He is a devoted father and husband, not yet 38 years old, and he has no information regarding the fate which has befallen his family. He therefore attempts to make his way back from the Albanian front by any means necessary. He begins his journey on horseback, then climbs aboard a lorry and travels with it until it runs out of petrol. When he reaches Niš – a city over 240 km away from Belgrade and the site of one of the first concentration camps on Serbian soil – he disposes of his uniform, as the Germans are arresting all the officers and murdering any Jewish ones on the spot. Now in civilian clothes, he climbs aboard a direct train towards the capital, but the Gestapo are already checking arrivals at the station and so, taking advantage of a moment when the train slows down as it approaches a curve in the tracks, he jumps from the wagon on the outskirts of Belgrade and proceeds on foot. When he reaches the family home and finds it demolished, he bursts into tears. There is no trace of the family. Sofia? The children? What has happened? Finally, one of the neighbours arrives and reassures him: his wife and children are alive and well, and they are waiting for him in his office. The wait is not over yet, however. The curfew makes wandering the streets too dangerous. It's not until the morning after when the Ladany family is whole again, held tight in an embrace.

That same day, father and grandfather decide that Serbia is no longer safe. Better off instead seeking refuge in Hungary. It is the easiest and most natural solution: the family has a Hungarian surname and all the Ladanys – adults and children – speak Hungarian. More importantly, the country is allied with Germany and is therefore not under Nazi occupation. When Serbia is partitioned following the invasion, Subotica and Novi Sad, the cities where Shaul's parents were born, are annexed back to Hungarian territory. There is only one obstacle in their path: reaching them means crossing the Danube, but all the bridges were destroyed in the bombings and the only way from one side to the other is aboard a boat or barge.

A few short hours after they are reunited, the Ladany family are on the riverbank, ready to be ferried across to a land they believe to be safer. 'The whole day, my sister and I are repeatedly reminded: it is forbidden to speak Serbian and even more forbidden to say that we are Jewish. As twilight falls, my grandfather approaches one of the ferry operators. In flawless Hungarian and in his most commanding voice, he says: "I am a retired Hungarian Royal State Railways employee, and I am taking my family home." His confident tone means that nobody bothers to check our papers, and by the following night we are already in Novi Sad, which has been rechristened Újvidék.'

Since 1919, Hungary has been governed by Admiral Miklós Horthy, a former Austro-Hungarian naval officer who came to power at the head of a nationalist-conservative coalition. The alliance with Germany is formalised in 1940, when Hungary becomes part of the Axis Powers, and Hungarian troops participate in the invasion of Yugoslavia in April 1941. According to a census from the same year, 825,000 Jews live in Hungary at the time; a figure which includes 100,000 converts to Christianity, who are considered Jews under laws passed between 1938 and 1941. All told, Jews make up less than 5 per cent of the overall population. The racial laws passed in Hungary are modelled on the German laws, and result in a gradual erosion of civil rights; mixed marriages are banned, certain professions are closed off, and Jews' participation in the economy is limited.

It is in these conditions that the Ladanys seek to rebuild their lives outside of Serbia. The scale of the challenge becomes clear almost immediately. Upon reaching Novi Sad, where they are hosted by the maternal side of the family, they are delivered another blow when Dionys is arrested and only released two days later thanks to the connections and influence of his father-in-law. The adults gather once more and decide that Novi Sad is no longer safe enough; better to put a greater distance between themselves and the Serbian border. Bags are repacked and once more it is time to leave. This time, the destination is Subotica (Szabadka in Hungarian), the city of Dionys' birth. 'Two of my grandfather's sisters live there in two

27

houses with a shared courtyard, which is basically a sealed-off complex. We live there for two months, during which time I am not allowed out even once. My father and grandfather, in the meantime, go to search for false documents that do not contain evidence of our lives in Serbia. My father is arrested twice during these expeditions, and, as he is a Jew, he is transferred to transit camps from where he would be deported to Germany. Both times, a former secondary school classmate who went on to become a senior police officer intervened to save his life, but after the second incarceration – which lasts for more than a week – we understand that not even Subotica is safe enough.' Any hope of a fresh start means another journey. The destination is Budapest.

THREE

A BOY, BUDAPEST AND EICHMANN

In 1941, Budapest is already a city with well over a million residents, and it appears to be the best place to hide in Hungary. The alliance with Germany guarantees the autonomy of the Hungarian government, but there is no shortage of oppressive measures against its Jewish citizens, afforded legitimacy by the racial laws that continue to expand over time. The Ladanys manage to obtain false papers which, despite confirming their religious identity, carry no reference to their status as refugees from Serbia. 'My father finds work as a researcher in a huge pharmaceutical centre, and then, once his shift is over, he works late into the night for two law firms specialising in patents, taking advantage of relationships he had built up previously with the lawyers managing them. Thanks to these two jobs, we have no financial troubles, and in October of that year, my parents are able to buy a large flat in a nice part of Buda.' A shade of normality which needs defending day after day. Jewish men are obliged to carry out forced labour, an imposition which originally affects only young men of suitable military age, but is later extended to all men deemed fit, beginning in 1940. 'My father is among the conscripts, but he can always get an exemption because his work in the pharmaceutical industry is considered vital.'

The Ladanys attempt to ensure their children have as normal a life as possible, so for the summer they send them to Monor, a town on the outskirts of Budapest where their uncle Imre is a practising lawyer. A different environment to the capital, but one that is no more immune to antisemitism: through the eyes of a 6-year-old boy, the mockery and cruelty of peers can be more difficult to understand than any number of regulations and clauses which make racism the law of the land. 'When they throw stones at you, when they call you "dirty Jew", you seek shelter and more than anything, you ask yourself "Why?" Why do the kids scoop up horse manure and throw it at you while you're walking with your sister? We're lucky to have my teenage cousin Vera there. She protects us and escorts us all the way into the courtyard of the house, where the perimeter walls provide sanctuary.'

These episodes leave their mark on Shaul, perhaps more than he himself realises. And they rise to the surface 45 years later in an Australian airport. 'The man at the check-in desk can't pronounce my name, so he repeats it two or three times, each time louder than before. Once we are done, a person standing behind me asks – in Hungarian – if I am also from Hungary. Without stopping to think, as if it comes from somewhere deep within me, I tell him, 'I'm Israeli. In Hungary I was just a dirty Jew.' I surprise myself: even in Germany I hadn't reacted so forcefully. But here it happened by instinct, it was almost a reflex.'

The cruel actions of the other children, unpleasant though they are, are nothing compared to what is happening outside Budapest, and the Ladanys have known about it for a while. The uninterrupted wailing one day of Sofia, Shaul's mother, is a tangible manifestation of the terror which surrounds them and the death which draws ever closer. The trigger for her tears is the news which has reached them from Novi Sad, where in January 1942 the Hungarian police and army organised a raid against members of the Resistance. It was an operation which soon turned into a round-up of thousands of Jews and other citizens. Those arrested were taken down to the banks of the Danube and shot, their bodies falling into its icy waters. Among the almost 4,000 victims of the massacre were Shaul's aunts – his mother's sisters – Peery and Margo, along with their husbands, the Zemanek brothers. Before they were captured, they took a precaution twhich is extreme for any parent: separating themselves from their children, who were between 12 years and 6 months old. They hid them away to give them a chance of survival. Hope had run out for the parents, but the children were later picked up by their grandparents, who would themselves end up facing the same firing squads, only to be saved by a countermand from Budapest which put an end to the massacre.

Grandma and Grandpa Kassovitz are now left to find a future for 12-year-old Olga, 6-year-old Evi, 4-year-old Robert, and Marta, born only 6 months previously and already orphaned. Olga stays with her grandparents, Robert goes to one of his mother's surviving sisters, Ila. That leaves Evi and Marta, who are entrusted to a non-Jewish person who conveys them to the Ladanys in Budapest. Evi is with them for two weeks before she is taken in by family members with no children of their own, while the youngest, Marta, grows up with Shaul and Shoshana. They know what happened to Marta's parents, but a decision is taken within the family not to talk about it: Marta is a daughter and a sister as far as all are concerned. And even though he is only 5-and-a-half years old, Shaul knows the importance of keeping a secret. Marta will discover the truth 20 years later, after Dionys' passing, when she is already a student at university. Someone plants the suspicion in her mind that the woman she calls *Ima* (Mum) might not be her real mother. Shaul intervenes. 'That was when I told her the truth. But she is still my sister today.'

The family grows, but the children's obligations remain the same. In September 1942, Shaul begins to go to school. For two years, he attends lessons in a class where he is the only Jew, a situation which becomes tragically dangerous from 19 March 1944, the day when German troops occupy Hungary. Germany is losing the war, and mistrust is increasing. The Hungarians are suspected of planning to sign an armistice agreement with the Allies, a risk which Hitler seeks to avoid. The result is Operation Margarethe, and when it concludes, Adolf Eichmann – head of Gestapo Unit IV B-4 and destined to become one of the most infamous war criminals of all time – is sitting in Budapest. Eichmann, who is living under the alias Ricardo Klement when he is captured by the Mossad in Argentina in 1960. Eichmann, the only person ever convicted under the death penalty by the State of Israel. Hanged, his ashes are scattered over the Mediterranean Sea, beyond Israel's borders.

'None of the significant, fundamental things that happened between 1935 and 1945 were my responsibility,' the former Obersturmbannführer Eichmann repeated over eight months of interrogations (from 29 May 1960–2 February 1961), 'because my rank and my position in the hierarchy were too low.' The professed modesty of a man who, in 1944, was awarded the War Merit Cross First Class with swords for his work serving the regime. Eichmann specialises in organising deportations, and in Hungary he demonstrates his capabilities. Within two months of his arrival in Budapest, he arranges over 145 transports, the majority of them to Auschwitz. In under 60 days of unflinching and clinical work, he sends 440,000 people to their deaths.

By the end of July 1944, the only Jews remaining in Hungary live in Budapest. Shaul's grandparents are forced to board one of those trains, along with his cousins Olga and Robert. All four of them had narrowly avoided the massacre in Novi Sad two years previously, but this time they have no means of escape. The final memory of his grandfather is a letter that reaches its destination some time later. An envelope left to fall from the moving train, with a few brief words alongside the name of its intended recipient: 'Whoever finds this letter is asked for an act of humanity, to find a way to deliver it to my family so that they may know the fate that has befallen us.' A prayer which is answered.

In 1961, Shaul is among the observers who queue up to enter Beit Ha'Am in Jerusalem (today the Gerard Behar Center) to offer support in the Eichmann trial. He wants to see the man whose signature sealed the fate of almost half a million people within a matter of days. He wants to see the accused who condemned Grandpa Max, to see the assassin who felt no pity even for children like Robert. 'My office was responsible only for deportations,' Eichmann would repeat, speaking about himself as if he were no more than a middle manager in a transport company.

In truth, in 1944 he was one of the most powerful men in Budapest, and the Hungarian capital was an increasingly dangerous place for its Jewish residents. His power over life and death is described by Enrico Deaglio, who recalls the meeting between Eichmann and Giorgio Perlasca in his book *The Banality of Goodness*. Padua-born Perlasca, later recognised as one of the Righteous Among the Nations, saved thousands of Jews by posing as a Spanish diplomat. Those helped by him included twins who were already on their way to board the trains which departed from Budapest's railyard. On that occasion, to save them from the concentration camps, Perlasca engaged in a heated argument with a German officer, who waved a pistol in his face to take the two young Jewish boys back. The argument continued until the arrival of a colonel who, in the face of the fake Spanish diplomat, signalled to his junior officer to back down. Then, turning to Perlasca, he quietly added: 'Keep them. The time will come. It will come for them too.' The colonel, who went unrecognised by the Italian, was Adolf Eichmann.

Those twins could easily have been the young Ladanys. Shaul's parents are aware of the danger and therefore decide to separate from their children in an attempt to protect them. The girls are entrusted to Christian friends of the family, while for Shaul they find an orphanage run by Salesian monks who don't ask too many questions. 'My father comes with me. The yellow star is sewn on to our coats, and when we reach the gates of the monastery, he removes mine, then his own, and holds them both in his arm so that only the linings are visible. Then he hugs me and gives me a kiss on the head: he doesn't say a word, and neither do I. We both know everything there is to know. He holds me close to him, but we don't cry. After a while, he rings the bell, and a priest appears. He doesn't ask any questions when my father tells him that I'm a boy for the orphanage. Then my father lets go of my hand and the gates close behind me: I can feel the tears coming, but I hold them back. I'm 8 years old.' A boy who, from that moment on, has to contend with a new kind of fear all by himself: being exposed. 'There are lots of kids in the orphanage, but I don't make friends with any of them, because I cannot risk them finding out that I'm Jewish. Soon it is Sunday, and when they tell me to go to chapel for the mass, I'm struck by terror: I'm sure to be found out there, because I don't have the faintest idea what to do during the service. I make up an excuse, tell them I'm a Protestant, but I'm not a good liar. And what if they take me to a Protestant church? What do I do then? I live with that fear every minute of every day. It's an uncontrollable terror that overwhelms me and forces me deep into my shell, which never happens again in my entire life.' Liberation comes two weeks later. It's not the same liberation that the whole of Europe is anticipating, but it feels the same to Shaul. The Allies have intensified their bombing campaigns over Budapest, and the bombs are falling so close to the monastery that his parents decide there is no point cutting themselves off from a child if the risk of death remains equally high. 'When my father comes to pick me up, I feel so happy, even though we go back home with the yellow star in full view on our coats.'

The return to the lodgings that the Ladanys call home lasts no more than a few days. There is not even time for Shaul to return to his previous places and activities before the entire family is forced to relocate to the ghetto. The order is delivered by an SS officer, accompanied by two members of the Luftwaffe, who move from room to room, indicating the things that are to be left behind. The residents of the house have 24 hours to leave. These are not yet the ghettos that will be established in autumn 1944, when the Horthy regime is removed from power. During this phase, a conviction takes hold among the Hungarian fascists (the Arrow Cross Party) that it would be better to distribute the Jews around the city, to use them as human shields and attempt to discourage the Allied bombing raids. In the space of a few short weeks, 200,000 people are moved from their homes, separated from their belongings, and packed into cramped living spaces. 'We were five in one room, and when we were transported, the Germans took all the best things we owned in the old house. In the meantime, my father is increasingly active in the community's Zionist movement.' Budapest is the birthplace of Theodor Herzl, the father of modern Zionism. The publication of his *Der Judenstaat* (The Jewish State) in 1896 made the philosophical case for a Jewish state, to put an end to antisemitic persecution. 'If you will it, it is no dream,' wrote Herzl a few years later in his book *Altneuland* (*The Old New Land*). These ideas have a powerful impact on Dionys Ladany during his university years in Karlsruhe. There are debates over the best place to give birth to this new state, if not in Palestine. There is talk of

Argentina, and then there is the Uganda Proposal. There are many ideologies, but for now it is not a matter of intellectual discussion among students, but one of survival. It is this renewed commitment by Ladany senior which will end up transforming his family's fortunes.

FOUR

BERGEN-BELSEN

Who is Rudolf Kastner? To Israeli judge Benjamin Halevi, he is a man 'who sold his soul to the devil'. It is Kastner who, in 1944, signs an agreement with Eichmann to buy safe passage for the Hungarian Jews. Ten thousand trucks in exchange for a million people: this is the initial plan, which ends up as nothing but a hangman's accounting trick. The trucks become money – large sums of money that desperate people are willing to pay in exchange for hope. What is the cost of a life? How much are your children worth? Is there anything you would not forfeit, to avoid death?

In 1944, as months pass, the Nazis begin to realise that the war is slipping from their grasp: on 6 June, the Allies land in Normandy. The end of the Third Reich is approaching and among the

German officials, there are those who are starting to look towards an alternative and equally prosperous future. In Budapest, Standartenführer Kurt Becher is working on the direct orders of Himmler. Through him, the SS has already taken ownership of over half the assets of the Weiss family, who, Eichmann would recall during his interrogation, controlled 'the most important industrial group in Hungary, in a way the Hungarian equivalent of the Krupp family'. A de facto expropriation, and one that sees 48 members of the Weiss family transferred to Portugal on board two German aeroplanes in exchange.

'There were often three-way conversations,' Eichmann continues, 'between Kastner, Becher and myself. The substance of these discussions was always the same: allocating quotas of Jews to be sent to Palestine and for whom Becher would receive a quid pro quo.' This is where the exact value of a human life is calculated, down to the nearest cent. A sort of nightmarish auction in which, Hannah Arendt writes, Eichmann offers a valuation equivalent to an end-of-season sale. 'There was considerable haggling over prices, and at one point, it seems, Eichmann also got involved in some of the preliminary discussions. Characteristically, his price was the lowest, a mere two hundred dollars per Jew; not, of course, because he wished to save more Jews but simply because he was not used to thinking big. The price finally arrived at was a thousand dollars, and one group, consisting of 1,684 Jews, and including Dr Kastner's family, actually left Hungary.'

Those 1,684 people include scientists, artists, leading representatives of the Jewish community and activists in the Zionist movements. Also on board was Shaul Ladany and his family. A boy, largely unaware of the negotiations taking place around him. 'At the exact moment that we are preparing to be transferred to an internment camp, the doorwoman for our building – a horribly antisemitic woman – calls two Hungarian policemen, thinking that my family are trying to escape. The two officers, seeing my father and I with suitcases in our hands, confront him and begin to beat him. When he falls to the ground, they kick him repeatedly. I stand there helpless, silent, while my father doesn't resist, knowing that if he did, they would shoot him. The beating continues for several minutes, and I am really worried that my father might be killed.' Salvation comes in the form of three German soldiers from the Wehrmacht: Dionys Ladany had paid them to escort the family to the camp, and they are the ones who interrupt the assault; whether out of concern for their payment or distaste for yet another unnecessary murder is unclear. They are moved to a camp on Columbus Street, but safety is still a distant prospect. 'We're separated into groups, to split up the departures: ours is the first, and it includes fewer than 2,000 people. My grandparents are part of the third group. We say goodbye to them on 2 July 1944: they are due to follow us a few days later.' However, negotiations between the Nazis and the Jewish representatives break down, and the initial 1,684 are the only ones to leave Hungary. The agreement calls for them to arrive in a neutral country, but the journey is anything but straightforward. It is marked by fear, where a few letters on a piece of paper can change your fate. Assent can be taken away and replaced with refusal, and the stubborn and obtuse ignorance of a functionary can lead to your death. 'We reach the Hungarian border at Magyarovar, where the station manager refuses to accept that our train is supposed to continue on to Auspitz, a small village in the Protectorate of Moravia. He is convinced there has been a mistake, and that our actual destination is Auschwitz. They hold us there for two days, until they receive further instructions confirming that our travel documents are correct.' This is not the only psychological torture inflicted on people who have been living trapped between doubts and fears for years. 'At Linz they lead us off the train and take us to the public bathrooms, to shower. My father has heard the stories of those who were in Poland, and whispers "gas" before he goes into the showers with great reluctance. Luckily, it's a false alarm: these are real showers.'

The showers were not a gas chamber, but two days later, the train journey ends at the open gates of Bergen-Belsen.

Built in 1940 as a prisoner-of-war camp, Bergen-Belsen gradually became a concentration camp: the Nazis initially used it to hold Jews whom they sought to trade in prisoner exchanges. In 1942, Himmler and the heads of the SS are no longer so intransigent in their pursuit of the Final Solution. The only good Jew is no longer a dead Jew, but also one who can be exploited. As Himmler himself wrote: 'All the Jews who have family in the United States in positions of influence are to be placed in a special camp . . . and kept alive. For us, these Jews are valuable hostages.' A dedicated area within Bergen-Belsen is set aside to hold these prisoners in April 1943. By 1944, however, things have changed. Other prisoners begin to arrive in Lower Saxony – first the sick and infirm, then those removed from concentration camps that are too close to the eastern front. Overcrowded and with the constant threat of outbreaks of disease, Bergen-Belsen too becomes an extermination camp, and it is no coincidence that in December 1944, Hauptsturmführer Josef Kramer – commandant of Auschwitz-Birkenau – is appointed to oversee the complex. A few weeks prior, a young German-born Dutch girl had also arrived at Bergen-Belsen from Auschwitz-Birkenau: Anne Frank. Aged 15, she was seven years older than Shaul. She died a few months after being transferred to the camp.

Shaul Ladany and his family are held in the camp between July and December 1944. 'Every single day of those six months is burned into my memory: the hunger, the rain, the cold, the endless rollcalls, the barbed wire and the electric fence, the guard towers and the SS officers who shout at us endlessly. I remember one in particular, who had a cleft lip. And then there were the smells; the unbearable stench from the toilets mixed with the scent of the tomatoes that grew beyond the electric fence. The plant has wound itself around the fence beyond, and

I can only watch as the tomatoes ripen. I cannot even bite into one to gain a temporary break from the overpowering and constant hunger. Eating becomes a constant source of anxiety. Despite this, I am aware that we are more fortunate than other prisoners: our group is permitted to wear civilian clothes, warmer than the uniforms worn by the others, and the adults are exempt from carrying out forced labour.'

Having your name appear on the lists of those destined to leave is no guarantee of safety. 'Around October or November, we are asked to declare our nationality. Immediately, people in the camp begin to discuss what they should be saying. Many people can choose from several options: we can define ourselves as Hungarian, Serb or Croat, for example. The fact is that how we choose to answer could determine our fate. In the end my parents decide to say we are Hungarian, while the Kassovitzes, family on my mother's side, decide to say they are Romanian. They are from Transylvania and also speak Hungarian, but believe they are better off associating themselves with Romania, where the King opposed the deportations of the Jews. They are wrong. When the Germans finally allow us to leave Bergen-Belsen, they hold back all of those who claimed Romanian citizenship, as punishment for Romania's defection from the Axis. While we are on our way to Switzerland, hunger and disease take the life of Bandy Kassovitz.'

Another train and another four days, with long stops where – inevitably – everyone fears being sent back to Bergen-Belsen. 'Then, at one point, a few men in uniform enter the carriage. They speak German, but they are polite towards us. It's the first time in a long time that I hear this language without it being shouted at me. We are in Switzerland.' A safe place which is not necessarily synonymous with freedom: the passengers on board what would later become known as 'Kastner's train' are taken to a refugee camp in Caux, near Montreux. When the Ladanys succeed in finding a place in Basel, the precise and punctilious Swiss present the family with the bill for their detention. 'The invoice includes a detailed list of all the expenses we incurred during the months we were under their charge, from the moment we crossed the border. It even includes a bar of chocolate they had given me on our arrival.' The permission to leave the camp and settle in Basel is also not without an ulterior motive: the Ladanys are permitted to move when Shaul's father agrees to become part of a working group led by Professor Tadeus Reichstein, without pay. 'My father is enthusiastic about his research, and he is even granted permission to patent a process for producing calcium gluconate under his own name, which will later be used in Yugoslavia, Israel, Czechoslovakia and Bulgaria. His greatest satisfaction comes in 1950, when Professor Reichstein is awarded the Nobel Prize in Medicine: my father kept the letter of thanks he received from the professor until his dying day.'

The senior Ladanys, Dionys and Sofia, remain in Basel with little Marta, while Shaul and Shoshana are sent to a boarding school. 'It was actually a summer camp, in Heiden, but during the war the Swiss Jewish community converted it into a permanent structure. There are about 200 of us there. Alongside us Hungarians there are also Polish and French children. And so I go back to school, almost a year after I last set foot in a classroom.' It is here, aged 9, that Shaul is introduced to long-distance walking for the first time. The occasion is a class trip to St Gallen for eye tests. The older students are invited to make the 32 km return journey on foot, and Shaul insists on tackling it alongside them. The others attempt to talk him out of it, but he is stubborn and refuses to listen. It's no Sunday afternoon stroll, a fact that his muscles remind him of at every step. Nonetheless, despite the pain, he makes it to their destination. School, walks, games: the time spent in Switzerland resembles a normal life, or as normal as can be for such a young child separated from his parents. On the one side is a family divided but determined to rebuild a future for itself, on the other is a Europe that slowly but steadily, week by week, is witnessing the advance of the Allied troops. As the end of the war grows nearer, so the dream of reclaiming their past life grows: for those who lived through the ghetto of Budapest and Bergen-Belsen, Basel is paradise. But it is not home. In the wake of Hitler's death and the fall of the Nazi regime, Dionys Ladany turns his attention back to Belgrade, to salvage the scraps of years of work. And to start over.

Returning to Yugoslavia is not easy. Train lines, bridges and roads everywhere have been destroyed by years of bombardments, and millions of people are on the move, either returning home or seeking a more peaceful life elsewhere. 'In September, we manage to find a place on a train leaving Switzerland. My sister and I go straight to the station from Heiden, and when my mother sees me coming, I can see she is annoyed, because a lot of my luggage is taken up with the vegetables that I grew in a small garden at the school. My suitcase is full of cucumbers and tomatoes, but what seems like a childish attachment to the fruits of my labour becomes a valuable gift, because the train journey lasts for two weeks. And there is no food on board.'

Much has changed in Belgrade since the Ladanys were forced to leave in 1941. Confidence needs to be regained in a city which has had its appearance altered beyond recognition by successive waves of bombing. The biggest surprise for the Ladanys comes when they reach their old house. The ground floor, where the grandparents had lived, is in ruins. The floor above it, however, where Shaul had lived with his family, is occupied by a new resident. 'The four of us are standing there on the landing with all of our possessions. My father decides to ring the doorbell. When he does so, a man comes to the door and my father introduces himself: 'My name is Ladany, I am the owner of this house. I have returned.' When he hears this, the man turns white, as if he is looking at a ghost or an alien. He probably knows that the house belongs to a Jew and has hoped that we will never show up again. Yet there we are, flesh and bone. Maybe because he feels guilty – most of the furniture, books and other objects have disappeared from our house – he lets us in. He lives in half of the flat, and in the other half – which is in ruins – he allows us to stay. If he had not been caught by surprise, any attempt, even a partial one, to regain ownership of our house would have been in vain and taking it through the courts would have been a long process. The way things turn out, we squeeze ourselves into the only room that is in semi-decent condition, and within four months we are able to restore the ground-floor unit and move in there. Some time later, a court order restores to us the grand piano that my parents had received as a wedding gift. It's a part of the family that makes the later journey to Israel with us and will ring out for decades to come in my mother's living room, delighting generations of grandchildren.'

The fight to regain a part of the possessions lost in the war is only just beginning. On 11 November 1945, the first post-war elections are held in Yugoslavia. Marshall Tito comes to power and gradually begins to forge his own vision of Soviet socialism, which includes a policy of nationalisation of the means of production. 'The biggest dispute surrounds my father's factory, which had been managed by the Germans during the war. He works hard and takes out a mortgage to rebuild and renovate the parts that had been destroyed, but about a month after production resumes, the communist regime comes to power and orders the nationalisation of the factory. There is no compensation or refund of any kind. On the contrary, they expect my father to continue to pay the mortgage, but he refuses, and a long legal battle begins. He will never have the factory back, but at least he will not have to submit to the extra insult of continuing to pay for its renovation.' Shaul has his own problems in those days. He is back at school once more, and this time he is unable to follow anything happening around him, because in four years he has completely forgotten his Serbian. 'Things become even more complicated when they begin to teach us another language in school. The language of the victors: Russian.' Another culture shock. And it won't be the last.

FIVE

THE PROMISED LAND

Change means a new alphabet to learn. First the Latin script, then Cyrillic, now it is the turn of Hebrew. Set to paper, the migration to the Middle East becomes a long string of unfamiliar characters that go from right to left. When the Ladanys make the decision to move to Israel, nobody in the family speaks Hebrew: Dionys is a Zionist, but he has a very limited relationship with Judaism. Sofia's edition of the Hebrew Bible, meanwhile, has the text in Hungarian alongside it. Only the most important holidays are observed at home – Yom Kippur and little else. On 14 May 1948, however, in Tel Aviv, David Ben Gurion proclaims the birth of the State of Israel, and when a family friend who has lived in Palestine for a while pays a visit to the Ladanys in Belgrade, Shaul's parents are convinced that – language or not – this is the place to settle and put down roots. This time there is no imminent danger facing them, but the urge to emigrate is powerful. 'Since our return to Serbia, we have not experienced antisemitism. Despite the nationalisation of the family business, my father has a good job as a researcher at the Institute of Food Science, and he is often sent on trips abroad by the government.' When Tito permits the Jewish residents of Yugoslavia to emigrate to Israel, the last remaining doubts disappear: the only condition placed by the Yugoslavian prime minister is that they leave behind everything of commercial or industrial value. The Ladanys sign away the rights to their property, and in early December they set sail from south of Rijeka, on the coast of Croatia, on board the *Kefalos*, a ship which is carrying another 4,000 people. 'The journey is dreadful and immediately begins on the wrong foot. Even when everyone is on board, we remain anchored for a week longer than was originally planned. Later, I found out that the delay was so that the ship could transport a shipment of weapons, evading an international embargo. The journey from Croatia to Israel should take four days, but we are at sea for two weeks, at the mercy of the waves, because the *Kefalos* is unstable and lurches dangerously. We are caught in a storm off the Greek coast, and when the engines stop working, the crew send out a Mayday signal, but nobody comes to rescue us. Once the fault is fixed, the journey continues and almost everyone suffers from seasickness: the floor is covered in vomit and our sleeping arrangements are in bunk beds that remind me of the ones we had in the shacks at Bergen-Belsen.' More than a year has passed since the infamous journey of the *Exodus 1947* and its passengers – boarded by British forces mid-voyage, the *Exodus 1947* passengers were sent back to Europe, first to France, then transferred behind barbed wire in British-run camps in Germany, before negative publicity and public pressure eventually saw their release. Even though the docking protocols have changed completely, the days on board the ship are yet another ordeal for those who have survived the Holocaust.

New immigrants are welcomed into the Promised Land in a cloud of DDT. The insecticide is sprayed on the clothes and bodies of those who disembark at the port city of Haifa: the date is 20 December 1948 and Israel is putting arrangements in place for its new citizens while simultaneously fighting the War of Independence to protect and uphold with force its right to exist. The Ladanys are first placed in a hostel in Be'er Ya'akov for a few weeks before being assigned accommodation in the city of Lod, a few kilometres from the airport. 'We are in two rooms without electricity or running water. There is not even a kitchen, and if we need the bathroom we have to go into the garden, in an outhouse that is shared with other families living in the same courtyard. My mother is despondent, and throughout this time she repeats over and over again: "What have we done? We have no money, and we are stuck in the middle of nowhere." My father tries to console her. He is convinced by the decision they have taken, and remains optimistic: this is our land, and through hard work we will succeed. A short time later, he decides to open a pharmacy.' Shaul in the meantime is trying hard to integrate, as all children do, by playing with the neighbours' children, who come from Poland, Romania and Bulgaria. 'Because I don't speak Hebrew, I get by with my Serbian, which works quite well with the Bulgarians, while my sister Marta spends her time with the Romanians and picks up some of their language.'

It is not only immigrants from Europe who arrive in Israel: over 650,000 Jews come from North Africa and the Middle East in those years to a country with fewer than 1.5 million people in total: 260,000 from Morocco alone, almost 130,000 from Iraq, 56,000 from Tunisia, tens of thousands from Yemen, Libya, Egypt, and so on down to the 6,000 who come from Lebanon and 4,500 from Syria. All people with a shared faith, but life experiences and cultures which are difficult to reconcile. What does a Jew born and raised in Berlin have in common with one who has spent their entire life in Baghdad? While the new society searches for answers, the war is still raging. At the very time the Ladanys are settling in their new homeland, the Israeli army is advancing through the Negev Desert as far as Eilat on the coast of the Red Sea, reaching it on 5 March 1949.

For many children like Shaul, the path to integration passes through school and the military: involvement in quasi-military activities begins at a young age. 'From the start of high school, we are taken on marches along the beach at seven in the morning, before lessons begin. It's part of the "Gadna" programme that the army organises to prepare and train future soldiers before they enlist. Ever since I heard about military academies like Saint-Cyr in France, I have dreamed of becoming an officer and it is my goal to pursue a career like this.' Shaul's aspirations extend beyond military life, however. His fluency in Hebrew is steadily improving, and at school he compensates for his initial difficulties with the language by excelling in maths and sciences. In addition to a career as an officer, he is increasingly drawn to the idea of following his father into becoming an engineer. Around the time when the moment of truth arrives and the important decision must be taken, Shaul wins a contest: for weeks he has been patiently filling out giant crosswords in a local newspaper, and of all the people who succeeded, his name is drawn to win a trip to Marseilles. The year is 1954, and Shaul goes on a little tour of Europe before he is drafted into the military. 'The year before I had visited Italy on a school exchange programme: in a few days we had visited Rome, Florence and Milan. We would leave one museum and go straight into the next one. This time I decide to visit France and Spain: from Marseilles I go to Paris, where a cousin of mine hosts me, and from there I go to Madrid (where I see my first and last bullfight), Barcelona, Mallorca and Valencia. When I return, I am ready to become an officer, even though deep inside I have already decided that that will not be my life. When I grow up, I want to be an engineer.'

The impact of life in the barracks further reinforces his decision. Military service is mandatory and tough, taking three years out of the life of kids who have barely turned 18. But none of this is what turns Shaul away from a life in uniform. 'Basic training in the Artillery Corps is easy for someone like me who has gone through the entire Gadna process, but one thing I cannot understand is the often stupid punishments. I even receive one myself, for improperly saluting a superior officer while I am in the mess hall with my rifle in one hand and the mess tin in the other. As punishment, I am ordered to report to the sentry on duty at one-hour intervals through the night in full combat gear and with my bed made. Another time, they order me to dig a large hole, a metre wide and deep . . . and then make me fill it in again as soon as I'm done. That is how I come to realise that I don't have the necessary mindset for a military career, because I don't like taking orders, especially unreasonable ones. Despite this, I work hard to become an officer and I succeed.' Military service consists of more than training exercises and punishments. In 1955, the borders of Israel are as fresh as they are dangerous, and Shaul finds himself deployed along the Gaza Strip alongside the other members of his battery. 'For four months we are on active duty with no leave. We are taken to a kibbutz to shower once every two weeks. One of my fellow soldiers, Gideon, is not even allowed to go home to attend the Shloshim of his father, the traditional day of mourning that marks a month since the passing of a loved one. Our mission is to provide cover fire for the border patrols. Every so often we are bombarded ourselves in exchanges of fire.'

After completing his first year of service, Shaul asks to postpone the remaining period in order to study. At first his request is approved, but a few weeks later he is recalled when Israel begins planning the Sinai Campaign. 'My request to return as an officer cadet is approved by the general in charge of the Israel Defence Force's training branch. The general is Yitzhak Rabin, a name which means very little to me at the time, certainly a lot less than it will later: in 1974 Rabin becomes prime minister for the first time, and in 1993, during his second term in office, he signs the Oslo Accords, shaking the hand of the leader of the Palestine Liberation Organisation (PLO), Yasser Arafat. Two years later, he is assassinated in Tel Aviv, not by a Palestinian but by Yigal Amir, a 25-year-old far-right Jewish extremist.'

Remarkably, this is already the second time in Shaul Ladany's life that his path has crossed that of a victim of an unspeakable homicide committed by one Israeli against another. While Shaul is undertaking his military service, in Jerusalem a trial is under way that involves Rudolf Kastner, the man who had signed the agreement with Eichmann. An old Hungarian Jew by the name of Malchiel Gruenwald had published a scathing accusatory pamphlet against Kastner and the case had wound up in court. What was at first intended as a trial to rule on the defamatory nature or otherwise of Gruenwald's text rebounded against Kastner, who began the legal process as the injured party only for the case to turn against him. In his verdict, the judge, Halevi (who would later preside over the Eichmann trial), was highly critical of Kastner. For some it was a moment of truth, for others a court- and media-driven lynching. 'More than the talks he held with Eichmann, people were not willing to forgive Kastner for testifying on behalf of Kurt Becher, the person in charge of all the concentration camps in Germany. This allowed Becher to avoid being put on trial at Nuremberg and to return to live and do business freely after the war. But Kastner's testimony was not offered in secret. On the contrary, the Jewish Agency – one of the largest and most pivotal organisations in the early days of the State of Israel – allegedly paid for his travel . . .' The last word on this controversial page in history is written on the night of 3 March 1957, when three men accost and fatally wound Kastner while he is returning to his home. This is the first act of politically motivated murder by one Jew of another to be carried out on Israeli soil. The three men arrested and sentenced for the crime (Ze'ev Eckstein, Dan Shemer and Yosef Menkes) are pardoned and released in 1963: a life term effectively commuted to a six-year sentence – in Israel there are those who wish to leave this story in the past, with all its painful wounds.

While the Kastner case continues to occupy the front pages, Ladany is still in the military, awaiting the start of his officer training course, when something happens that will change his life for ever. It is fairly unremarkable, almost incidental, but is the moment when Ladany discovers a passion for running: 'For the first time in months I have some free time, and I decide to use it to run laps of the base, round and round for 25 km. After a bit of training, I get the idea into my head that I can do a marathon: on one of the weekends when I'm not on base, I try –

patching together a course around my house. I'm so inexperienced that I set off at about midday, and after 32 km I'm completely exhausted and dehydrated. I stop and use the little money I have to take a taxi back. The next week I decide to try again, and this time I don't even take any small change with me, so I cannot give in to the same temptation again. I hold out until the 37th kilometre . . . I'm only five short of the finish line I had set for myself, but again I am unable to finish. The taxi? I find a way around the problem: I stop one and tell him I will pay him as soon as I get home. It works.' A second failure does not deter Shaul. He has got it into his head to run the 42.195 km marathon distance, and so the following week, he tries for the third time in a row: this time in an official competition. 'On the Thursday, with my legs still hurting from the two failed attempts, a friend shows me a short piece in the newspaper, just three lines: *Saturday at 6.00 am in Hadera, the first official marathon organised by the State of Israel.* I don't think twice before deciding to take part. I switch my guard duties with one of the other soldiers, and I hitchhike to Hadera the evening before the race. I discover that there are eight of us competing, and the only one who has done any proper training is a man by the name of

Shalom Kahalani, who will go on to win it in a time of 2 hours and 41 minutes. Only two of the other participants cross the finish line behind him, while all the others, including me, are forced to retire. My race ends at the 35th kilometre. I'll have to try again.'

SIX

SHOSHANA

There is no expectation that a future racewalker should also be a good marathon runner. The problem is that Shaul's introduction to racewalking also leaves something to be desired. 'In the summer of 1956, after a lot of running training, I hear that the army magazine *BaMahane* is organising a 3 km racewalking competition in Tel Aviv. I'm used to doing far more than that on my weekends at home, so I decide this should be a stroll. I keep it to myself, but I think I could finish among the leaders, and who knows, maybe even win.' Of course, it requires a degree of comfort with the technique – racewalking is more than a matter of simply walking and wiggling your hips. There are two fundamental rules: both feet must never be detached from the ground at the same time, as this would constitute running, which is a breach of the rules. And then there is the matter of the knees, which must be locked, with a stride that resembles military parades. Heel-and-toe, heel-and-toe, heel-and-toe . . . the dialogue with the road starts from the feet – use them properly and you are halfway there. Once the technique has been acquired, it becomes time to factor in the distance. A 3 km track race means seven-and-a-half laps, with everyone starting at the same time at the sound of the starting pistol, and the rest is down to natural selection. 'The first two laps are no problem, even though I'm already wheezing. I keep in touch with the leading group through the third and fourth laps, but the exhaustion is almost unbearable. By the fifth lap, I simply cannot keep up with them any more. Completely humiliated, I retire.'

Anyone else would seek another hobby in the face of such a lacklustre and disappointing initiation. What is the point of carrying on with the charade? Even more so when the next attempt at tackling a marathon also falls short of the finishing line: this time the race is a qualification event for the Melbourne Olympics. Even if he were to qualify, it is unlikely Shaul could travel to compete in Australia. In autumn 1956, he and the other officer cadets are called up ahead of the Sinai

Campaign. 'When the war is over, we are awarded a decoration, even though we did not have an active part in the combat. On one of my weekends off, I decide to hitchhike to see the places where they were shooting until a few days before. I get to Abu Ageila, and the scene surrounding me is not pleasant. That year, I finish my military service and I am officially a second lieutenant of the Artillery. Now I can dedicate myself to my studies.'

The first months at the Technion are not easy. By the time Shaul arrives, the semester is almost halfway done. He also has approximately 100 classmates, and not one of them is female. 'The few female students at the university are not exactly beautiful. The only exception is Dina Hoffman, but she studies electrical engineering, and I have chosen mechanical engineering. They have a reputation for being so unfeminine and unattractive that it is said that Israeli women can be divided into three categories: beautiful, ugly . . . and those who study at the Technion.' While attractive company may be at a premium, enjoyment is not: his summer job at a factory means that, in his third year of university, Shaul can purchase a Vespa, which allows him to go sightseeing around Israel. Together with a group of around 20 friends, Saturdays are declared beach days in Herzliya: even in midwinter, he and his friends throw themselves into the sea and swim. It becomes such a proud tradition that one of the members of the group, Yossi Levine, issues membership cards for the Winter Swimmers Club. Then there are the tenth anniversary celebrations of the founding of the city of Eilat, when they organise a motorcycle convoy and travel across the Negev Desert. 'During the way back, Naomi Zisman, who is riding on my Vespa, decides to move over to Shimaleh's sidecar. Feeling faint from the heat and with no one to talk to, I attempt the impossible: I decide to see whether it is possible to ride while asleep. I succeed. Although I wake up immediately when I fall at the side of the road. I am unhurt, except for a few scratches and bruises. The Vespa is slightly damaged, but still works. My friends decide to move one of the girls back to ride with me as far as Tel Aviv. Just to make sure I don't fall asleep again.'

The most memorable summer comes in 1959. Shaul is accepted on to an exchange programme for engineering students: he is set to work in a paper mill in Apeldoorn in the Netherlands. 'I choose the cheapest way to travel: I buy a ticket on board a ferry to Greece – from there I take the train to Austria and from there I hitchhike all the way to the Netherlands. In the Netherlands I am given a bicycle for travelling between the house where I am living and the factory, and I decide to use my new mode of transport to explore the country. I mark a 90km route on my map and spend the weekend pedalling: all the training I have done means I have no problems with my muscles in the following days but . . . I cannot sit down for a week. A while later, Dania, my neighbour from Israel, joins me in Apeldoorn. When I am finished working there, we spend two months hitchhiking around Europe together with Uri, who has come over on the same programme as me and has been in Rotterdam. We go through Belgium, France, England and then all the way up to Scotland. The only money we spend is on the ferry across the Channel – for everything else we live on a budget of a dollar a day each.

'On our way back, we leave Dania behind in Paris and carry on through Switzerland to Italy, where my acting career very nearly takes off. It all happens by chance: producers from Dino De Laurentiis' production company show up at the youth hostel where we are staying, looking for new extras and new faces. During my travels around Europe, I have grown a beard, and they decide I would be perfect for the role of a sailor. They offer me a lot of money, and the idea of appearing in a film is very tempting: the problem is that if I sign the contract, I would be committing to spending three months on set, which would mean missing the last year of university and giving up the teaching-assistant position I have been promised. I reluctantly turn down the opportunity to become a film star.'

No Hollywood, not even a brief fling with Cinecittà Studios, but another surprise lies just around the corner for Shaul when he returns to Israel. Within 11 months of the most free-spirited summer of his youth, the life of the young man is going to change forever. It all begins with an unremarkable excursion in December 1959. 'I sign up for a day trip with the Society for the Protection of Nature in Israel, from Kfar Vitkin to Caesarea, and among the group that gathers on the Saturday morning I immediately see three cute girls standing together, and I go over to talk to them. One of them stands out in particular: no jewellery, no nail polish, lipstick or other make-up. She is a bit shy, but sweet and intelligent. Her name is Shoshana. We start to talk, and then we keep talking throughout the whole trip: we went to the same secondary school, but she is two years older than me and has already graduated with a degree in biochemistry from Hebrew University. Now she is studying for a PhD in endocrinology. I have no idea what that means, but she explains it to me in simple words that even an idiot like me can understand. Once the hike is over and she is standing there, waiting for the bus to Tel Aviv, I decide to be courageous and invite her to watch a film together. She doesn't say no; she says she already has plans to go to the opera, if she isn't too tired. My relationship with music is not the best – I have spent the years since childhood avoiding piano lessons at all costs – but that should not be an issue: I decide that opera isn't so bad and offer to take her on my Vespa. All I have to do is to run the 12 km back to where I left it in Kfar Vitkin. She whispers something that sounds like a yes, and I set off. But when I come back, an hour later, there is nobody at the bus stop. And I don't even know her surname or where she lives. I go home, change clothes, and immediately go to the theatre, hoping to find her there, but there's no trace of Shoshana. I am left with no choice but to go to my friends and tell them about my unbelievable day. The next morning, I still cannot get her out of my head, and so I set about finding her. My only lead is the secondary school, and so by 8 o'clock I am in the secretary's office making up an excuse to see the archives. I say that my older sister is looking for a former classmate. They let me look over the yearbooks, and finally, there she is: Shoshana Ahlfeld. Now I only have to look through the Tel Aviv telephone book, which is still very slim because very few people have telephone lines at home. I call the number, introduce myself and speak to her mother: Shoshana is not at home as, during the week, she lives and studies in Jerusalem. I ask for her address so that I can write to her.' Shaul sends her a letter declaring his intention to come and visit the following weekend: his words fail to reach her in time, and when Shoshana's mother tells her daughter about the telephone call, she mentions someone called Shmuel who rang up, looking for her.

It is not Shmuel, however, but Shaul, who shows up at her door the following Saturday. Shoshana is speechless. Eleven months later, on 6 November 1960, they are husband and wife. 'And if it had been up to him, we would have been married sooner,' says the woman who spent the next 58 years by Shaul Ladany's side. In the mind of the groom-to-be, it is already clear that this woman is the one, and there is no need to waste any more time. He knows. Full stop. He is also able to convince the two families, aided by the fact that Ladany and Ahlfeld seniors are already acquainted. They were both members of the Zionist movement during their university years in Germany, and they share many friends and memories. However, the Ahlfelds' journey to Israel differed from that of the Ladanys.

Shoshana has German roots; she was born in Nordhausen and arrived in Palestine before the Declaration of Independence. In Germany, her father Ludwig was an architect who took over the large family shop following the passing of her grandfather. The display windows of the shopfront are targeted by the Nazis on Kristallnacht in 1938. 'A family friend warned us that we would be targeted,' recalls Shoshana, 'so we hide in the attic, while Jews are being threatened and attacked and having their belongings destroyed all over the city.' It has become too dangerous to stay, and so the Ahlfelds decide to leave, but the British are accepting only a limited number of Jewish migrants in Palestine. There is one exemption, however; for applicants who can prove that they have a bank account holding at least £1 million. The family's fortune is insufficient to ensure the safe passage of everyone – uncles, aunts and cousins – and so the Ahlfelds embark on a deception: staggering their departures and moving their money from one family's account to another's, so satisfying the British. In truth, there was not a whole lot of money there.

And so, in 1939, Shoshana and her parents set sail from Italy: with the threat of Nazi violence behind them, it is not easy to forge a new home in a land that is not yet a state. Jews and Palestinians both live under the British Mandate, and it is difficult to integrate and assimilate. 'At first, we lived with family members,' says Shoshana, 'then my mother moved to Tel Aviv in search of work. In Germany she had continued her studies even after graduation and she was qualified to teach foreign languages, but in a situation like theirs now, any work would do. There's a letter she wrote to my father, which I kept with me, where she says: "I'm so happy, I've finally found work as a cleaner and dishwasher."' From the bottom, it is time to rebuild.

The first years of married life are also frugal for Shaul and Shosh, as he has always called her. They have both taken the decision to pursue their studies – she with the PhD and he enrolling in a master's programme in mechanical engineering, followed by another in business administration. 'It's a new field, one I know next to nothing about. The first course opens in 1961, and the following year I am part of only the second group of students to study this field.' To make ends meet, the two newlyweds rely on Shoshana's academic grant and Shaul's position in charge of the maintenance workshop at the Hebrew University. When the university undergoes a restructuring process, Shaul Ladany is afforded an opportunity to make a symbolic contribution to the nascent State of Israel: he is entrusted with supervising all the electromechanical components of the Knesset, the new parliament building under construction in Jerusalem. 'I learn a lot about the worst of human nature during that time: confusion caused by greed, arrogance, lust for power and fame. The original project is constantly being revised to make sure someone else gets their slice of the cake, and the costs slowly balloon.

'I remember a story I was once told by the speaker of the Knesset, Reuven Barkat, that I find helps to understand: "When God created Man, He wanted to make him perfect. He thought about the most important qualities to give him and decided on three: he should be blessed with intelligence, honesty and political skills.

When Satan heard what God was planning, he sought to persuade Him not to create such a man, as it would not leave any room for diabolical activity. God accepted his argument and they settled on a compromise: every man would possess only two of those traits. From that day on, any honest man who goes into politics cannot be intelligent; if he is intelligent and goes into politics, he cannot be trusted. And if he is smart and honest . . . he doesn't go into politics."

SEVEN

NEW YORK CITY

'Roll up the windows and lock the doors: we are now approaching Harlem.' The voice, speaking in an accent Shaul and Shosh find almost impossible to understand, belongs to a New York taxi driver. They have landed stateside.

The year is 1965, the United States has lost JFK, and people are listening to the final speeches of the Reverend Martin Luther King Jr while President Lyndon B. Johnson sends the best of the nation's youth to their deaths in Vietnam: 58,169 Americans will die; their average age only 23 years old.

Shaul and Shosh Ladany are yet to celebrate their fifth wedding anniversary when they find themselves together with their suitcases on the pavement outside Woodbridge Hall, on the corner of 115th and Riverside Drive, the residence that Columbia University reserves for married students.

The opportunity to emigrate for a few years began with a PhD: Shaul has been offered the opportunity to further specialise in his chosen field, studying business administration at Columbia. The proposed scholarship is less than what was originally proposed, but the prospect of moving to the States is too exciting to turn down. And so it is without regrets that Shaul leaves the job he had taken at a sewing-machine factory and departs with Shoshana. They fly from Israel to Greece, cross the Balkans and the Alps by train as far as Luxembourg, then take another flight with a stopover in Iceland. All told, the journey to New York takes three weeks. 'It was the cheapest way, and therefore the best, considering that all we had beyond my scholarship was Shoshana's salary for her job as a researcher at the Columbia School of Medicine.'

The young couple know almost nobody in New York. Their only contacts are the lady Shaul calls Aunt Trude – the childhood governess of the Ladany household – and Henry Laskau, the American racewalker Shaul had met during the Maccabiah Games, the Olympics-style event that brings together Jews from around the world. This sporting friendship had been struck up during the years between the end of Shaul's military service and the couple's departure to the USA, by which time Shaul had become a recognised athlete. Those initial doomed marathon experiments were a distant memory; a warning not to lapse back into draining his energy before the finish line. From 1957 to 1965, Ladany laid the foundations of his professional sporting career, first as something of a celebrity at amateur events and later as a pioneer of track and field in Israel.

It all began with the Four-Day March, a military exercise that the Israeli army decided to open up to civilians: participants march for 40 km each day, sleeping in camps set up for the occasion. Thousands of people attend and there is a festive spirit, with music and dancing by the light of bonfires in the evenings. 'I take part every single year, starting in 1957, first as a carefree participant with friends from the Technion, later allowing myself to be swept up in the competitive spirit. I win my first stage in 1959, on the second day of marching: a success that immediately motivates me to try again, because there are a lot of journalists there to greet me and my interview is broadcast live on the radio. A triumph. The next day, though, my legs are aching and one of them is swollen, which is a reason to worry: there is no encore. On the last day, in increasing pain, I cross the finish line a long way behind the leaders.' Another useful experience to help him to understand how to tackle such events. Over the years that follow, Shaul Ladany becomes the undisputed star of the Four-Day March, so much so that following the 1962 event, he decides to push himself further. 'After seeing my performance, someone says to me that I could even win the national racewalking championship, and so, at the first opportunity, I decide to try. The race takes place at the Hebrew University Stadium over a distance of 3 km: I win by almost a whole lap.' With victory, the sporting career of Shaul Ladany officially took off, until – three years later – racewalking is his ticket to exploring the United States.

'The day after our arrival in New York, I decide to call Henry Laskau. I don't know what to expect from a person who has only met me in passing. But when I call him, he is immediately very warm and friendly: he tells me that there is a race taking place that weekend, and so I spend my first American weekend on the march. The journey there is a little adventure of its own, because there is no mention of the event in the *New York Times*, so I show up in

Atlantic City at dawn on the Sunday without ever having been there before and with no idea when and where the starting line might be. Luckily, I find a police station: they give me directions, and soon after that I am in a changing room, waiting for the start with about 80 other racewalkers.' Ladany finishes his first race on American soil in 13th place, ahead of John Shilling, a dentist from Long Island and one of many competitors from that day who would become his friend. He had found a family among the Stars and Stripes: a group of men who rack up the kilometres with their rolling stride, all locked knees and rotating hips. Now all he needs is a team to compete with and things can really get going.

The most important sports club in the New York area is the New York Athletic Club (NYAC). Founded in 1868, its story is inseparable from the history of sport in the USA. Its athletes have won over 150 Olympic gold medals, the NYAC introduced cycling and fencing to the country, and it organised the first genuine athletics championships here. Most importantly, despite retaining an amateur ethos, it is one of the few organisations that provide its athletes with financial support for training and competitions. It's the ideal solution for a student like Shaul with limited resources.

But not everyone is convinced: 'They'll never accept you', Henry Laskau warns him firmly. His friend's pessimism is not rooted in sporting considerations: the response has more to do with background and skin colour. The United States is still deeply immersed in racial segregation and division, even in the democratic and multi-ethnic landscape of a city such as New York. 'In theory, there is no written rule that bars black and Jewish athletes from the NYAC. In practice, though, it doesn't happen. They admit a few, just enough to counter accusations of racism. And they already have the Jew they need to silence the critics: I often see him at the gym in Columbia. His name is Don Spero, he's a world champion rower who is studying for a PhD in physics.'

No New York Athletic Club then, so Shaul turns instead to the New York Pioneer Club (NYPC), the first multiracial club in the USA. It is not only Jews who are welcome here, but also blacks. Among Ladany's teammates is a man destined to go down in history, not only for his athletic abilities but also as the symbol of an era, all thanks to one simple gesture: a closed fist raised to the Mexico City sky. That moment in 1968 cements John Carlos as part of the iconography of the 20th century, bringing the black American protest movement to the podium of the Olympic Games. For Shaul, the sprinter is one of many athletes training with people like Joe Yancey and Ed Levy, the team's head coaches. It was here that Carlos, a young man of Cuban heritage who had grown up in Harlem, began the journey that earned him a scholarship at East Texas State University. It was in Texas that the sprinter would come to understand how much further there was to travel on the road to integration, despite the efforts of the Reverend King.

The NYPC is the perfect fit for Shaul, who begins to make a name for himself in the USA, race by race. He carries inside him the verdict that had been passed down on him a few months earlier by Mordechai Magali, a coach with the Athletics Committee of the Israeli Sports Association: 'You're 29, too old to become a good athlete.' Not only does Shaul continue to make progress, he is even starting to harbour Olympic dreams. 'In the United States I often have the opportunity to train with and race against athletes who have participated at Olympic Games or who hope to. And so, as my results gradually improve, I let myself catch the Olympic fever, too.' The prescribed cure for this condition is an extraordinarily large dose of kilometres, such as in April 1966, when Shaul decides to take on 200 laps of the track at Point Pleasant. The occasion is the 50-mile distance of the US Eastern Regional Championship, and not only does the 'old' Israeli win, he completes the race in a time of 8 hours 35 minutes and 35 seconds, breaking a US record that has held since 1878. After this achievement, the *New York Times* sends a journalist and photographer to the Columbia gym to meet Shaul and to write a feature about him. *Sports Illustrated* also takes an interest, with a short profile in the regular 'Faces in the Crowd' feature, dedicated to emerging athletes. The year before, the same pages were celebrating a 17-year-old basketball player called Lew Alcindor from Harlem, tall even by his sport's standards, who played for the Power Memorial Academy and became known as Kareem Abdul-Jabbar, the LA Lakers legend. This time, the face picked out from the crowd belongs to Shaul Ladany, who earns the honour 'for breaking the longest-standing US track record'. The race to the Olympics is on.

Racewalking in Israel is one thing, doing it in New York something else entirely. There are no half-empty roads winding through the desert, and in winter the cold becomes unbearable. Traffic and weather are not the only risks for someone training around the corner from Harlem, in the Bronx. In 1966, New York is experiencing two homicides a day, six sexual assaults and 700 thefts. Not exactly the safest place to be. 'Together with my friend John Kelly, an Irishman who grew up in New Zealand and tried a bit of everything when it came to sports, from boxing to the hammer, we decide to do a 50 km training session, doing laps around the Yankee Stadium. It's a horrible day, -10 ºC with 65km/ph winds, and we struggle to carve a path through the snow. I'm dressed for an expedition to Siberia more than for a racewalk: two pairs of socks, two pairs of tracksuit trousers, three shirts, a raincoat, two wool caps, two pairs of gloves and a scarf tucked into my collar. The padding comes in useful when a group of local thugs show up in front of us: they have seen us go past, then go past again, and they have obviously decided to prove to us that they are the kings of the road. They stand in a line in front of us, one next to the other, as if to say: "Now you have to stop." With John next to me, we don't take too long to make a decision: we speed up and head straight for them. Maybe they were not expecting us to react like that, because we catch them by surprise and when the moment of impact comes, they are the ones who hit the ground, while we continue marching without turning around. By the following lap, we're ready for Round 2, but there's nobody there any more. We finish training five-and-a-half hours later, covered in ice and sleet and resembling a pair of polar bears.'

The New York life of the Ladanys is taken up by training and studying, with Shoshana often accompanying Shaul to his races at the weekends. She takes a scientific approach to her husband's competitions. Literally. While Shaul is walking towards his goals, she dedicates herself to her research, making the most of her free time to leaf through books and review notes. Then, when he needs her support, she closes everything, fills a bottle with Coca-Cola and glucose, and passes it over to her favourite racewalker. On the track, too, they make an effective and harmonious team.

'We are happy in New York, despite our modest lives. No car, no TV, no cinema, no restaurants. One of the few times we go out to dinner, it's because we are invited to one of those conventions where you are given food while they try to sell you things. Generally, we don't go out much in the evenings: we try to get by on one of our two scholarships, setting aside a bit of money for when we go back to Israel. We like the city because, living there, you always have the feeling that you can find anything you want there, whatever you're interested in. Love Polynesian art? If you look, you'll be sure to find something. That's New York for me and Shosh.'

While their studies are ongoing, tensions are rising inside and outside Columbia University: the hippie movement is preparing for the summer of 1967, which will be remembered in the history books as 'the Summer of Love', with over 100,000 people gathering in San Francisco. As a foreign student, Shaul is an outside observer: he could not reasonably be described as a flower child, but he too was engaged in a highly specific battle against the formalistic dress code. 'From the day I arrived, the other Israeli PhD students would tell me about all the things that you could or could not do at the School of Business. Above all, I was told never to go to Professor Richmond's lessons without a jacket and tie. One time someone dared to, and the effect was scandalous; the professor told the person sitting next to the fearless offender to move away from him, for his own benefit – so that he wouldn't have to suffer the sight. The problem is that I hate ties and have always refused to wear them, except in really exceptional situations. I decide to go without, including for class, and Professor Richmond

Shaul with his sister Martha (left) and cousin Evi (right) in 1956, while on leave from officer training school. They are on the terrace of his parents' house in Ramat Chen.

Shaul with his parents, Dionys Ladany and Sofia Kassovitz, on the terrace of their house in Ramat Chen in 1957.

Shaul and Shoshana in 1960.

Adolf Eichmann listening as the court declares him guilty on all counts at his war crimes trial in Jerusalem, 1961. *Central Zionist Archives, courtesy of USHMM Photo Archives*

Training in New York City: at the Columbia University gym in 1966.

Refreshments during the 100-mile championship in Columbia, Missouri, 1967.

Shaul's feet after 50 miles of the 100-mile championship in Columbia, Missouri, 1967.

Walking alone from Jerusalem to Beer-Sheva via Bethlehem and Hebron, April 1968.

The 1969 Maccabiah podium for the 10-kilometre racewalk.
From left to right: Reuven Peleg, Shaul Ladany and Howie Jacobson.

West German policemen wearing sweatsuits, bullet-proof vests and armed with submachine guns, take up positions on September 5, 1972 on the Munich Olympic Village rooftops where armed Palestinians were holding Israeli team members hostage. *Press Association*

The team assembling at Munich Airport before the El-Al return flight with the coffins, to shake the hand of West German Foreign Minister, Walter Scheel. *CNN*

Competing at Tour du Var, France, 1974.

The finish line is close: Shaul is going to win the second stage of the Tour du Var, France, 1974.

Still King of the Road: a 50km walk with the author in the Negev desert in 2011.

In Rome in 2016, a shy Antonella Palmisano (left) asked Shaul to sign her copy of *Five Rings and One Star*. In 2021 she became an Olympic gold medallist in racewalking (also pictured is Elisa Rigaudo, who took bronze in Beijing 2008).

doesn't say a word. In the 1966/67 academic year I become his assistant, and later, he would become my dissertation supervisor.'

At the beginning of March 1967, news breaks that sends shockwaves through Columbia. It is discovered that the university is involved in projects being funded by the Department of Defense. The students and the pacifist movement take to the streets. It's the start of months of protests and rallies. 'One day I'm leaving the library, and right in front of me I see mounted police officers getting ready to charge the crowds that have gathered. I only just manage to escape without getting hurt.' The protest leads to the occupation of the university building, but what remains engraved in Shaul's mind is a sentence which appears one day on the wall outside the subway station: 'Lee Harvey Oswald, where are you now that we really need you?' President Lyndon B. Johnson reached the end of his term of office, fit and healthy, in 1969. He died of a heart attack at his ranch in Texas in 1973, while the Marines would not leave Vietnam until two years later.

EIGHT

EIGHT THOUSAND KILOMETRES, SIX DAYS OF WAR

Jerusalem, not Saigon: while the conflict in Vietnam limps on, Israel is also drawing closer to a war which seems increasingly imminent and unavoidable. In New York, Shaul and Shoshana study and work while constantly awaiting news.

'We shall not enter Palestine with its soil covered in sand, we shall enter it with its soil saturated in blood.' Declarations such as this – by Egypt's President Nasser – only add fuel to the fire, and words rapidly escalate to actions. In November 1966, Egypt and Syria sign a mutual defence agreement, and in the months that follow, every Israeli step feels like the spark that could set off a war. From the Arab perspective, such a conflict has a clear goal, described in unequivocal terms by the president of Iraq, Abdul Rahman Arif: 'The existence of Israel is an error which must be rectified. This is our opportunity to wipe out the ignominy which has been with us since 1948. Our goal is clear – to wipe Israel off the map.' Egypt, Syria and Jordan are on the frontlines, but the entire Arab world stands ready to support them. The Israelis cannot count on a similar level of support from the Americans, whose attention is directed firmly towards South-east Asia.

The event that triggers the Six Day War is later traced back to a flawed intelligence briefing: on 13 May 1967, the Soviets inform Egypt that the Israeli army is deploying ten brigades along its northern border in preparation for an attack on Syria. Damascus has received similar information, but there is no truth in the rumours – which would involve moving almost half of the Israeli army. Nasser decides to take action, and on 14 May 1967, two Egyptian armoured divisions move into the Sinai Desert, which leads to the first skirmish with Israeli tanks. On 16 May, Egypt calls on the United Nations to withdraw its troops from the region. Four days later, the Israeli government mobilises its reserve soldiers. On 21 May, Nasser orders a blockade of the Straits of Tiran.

'I try to keep up to date with the situation through the American media and a weekly edition of the Israeli

Ha'aretz newspaper that offers a kind of summary of the latest details on a thin sheet that's like cigarette paper. We can follow the latest developments almost in real time, and when I hear about the mobilisation, I immediately call the embassy in Washington to ask if I'm needed. They tell me that the army itself will get in touch if they need me. Not satisfied with this response, I write to the head of the Artillery corps, Colonel Israel Ben-Amitai, informing him that I am willing to return. In the meantime, as the situation gets worse by the hour, I volunteer to watch over the El Al airplanes at Kennedy Airport, to prevent potential terrorist attacks. Three days later, war breaks out.'

On 4 June, the Israeli government convenes to discuss its next steps, and by a split decision, votes in favour of taking action. By late morning on 5 June, the Egyptian air force has been decimated – runways and logistics infrastructure rendered useless – while the Israeli army advances through the Sinai Desert and on towards the Suez Canal. On the eastern front, the Jordanians attack and Israel retaliates, seizing control of East Jerusalem and the West Bank.

'The fighting starts, nobody calls me up to active service, but I decide to go anyway. However, all the flights to Israel have been cancelled. Because I worked at JFK, I know there is a cargo plane leaving within a few hours and I decide to try and board it. I call Shosh to let her know: I don't need too many words to convince her that I'm doing the right thing. If I don't go, I wouldn't be able to look at myself in the mirror.' Shaul prepares himself for war. 'I ask Shosh to buy me a kitbag, khaki clothes and tinned food, while I go to a sporting and hunting goods store on 42nd Street. I know the army is very disorganised when it comes to providing equipment for reservists, and I don't feel like that should be the reason I put myself in danger, so I decide to buy a semi-automatic rifle, some ammunition and a knife. I add a couple of gas masks to the collection. After the Egyptian attacks against the royalists during the war in Yemen, the possibility of chemical warfare can no longer be discounted. One mask is for me, the other I will give to my mother.'

A kiss for Shoshana, and Shaul is back at the airport. Two others who have also decided to try and return to Israel are there with him: one is a captain in the paratroops, the other is the nephew of chief of staff Yitzhak Rabin. The crew lets the men board, and they take their seats. 'No passport checks, no check-in. We just get on board and sit down in two long rows of seats between the flight deck and the cargo hold. It might seem strange, but the journey to war is far more comfortable than many other flights I've taken. Because it's not a jet, the journey takes longer than usual, but half a day later we land in Europe. It's dark outside, but as far as we can tell, we're in an airport near Rome. An official in plain clothes who speaks Hebrew and Italian comes to pick us up, and we follow him: no plaque on the door of his office, no clues that there are Israelis inside. It's clear that this is a regular site for stopovers, kept secret like the ships which left Italy with migrants on board in the days before Israel's independence. We go with him to refresh ourselves and return without anyone asking us for documents or anything else on the way. And a few hours later we leave again on board a different plane: a Boeing 377 Stratocruiser. This plane is clearly used for meetings and for transporting diplomats, because in the cabin where we are sent there is a long, horseshoe-shaped couch. We take the opportunity to sleep for a bit before we disembark in Israel.'

From the airport in Tel Aviv, Shaul immediately reports to the Artillery command, where Colonel Shdemati decides to second him to a technical intelligence unit: using aerial photographs, they are tasked with identifying Egyptian army outposts and sabotaging them beyond repair. 'Before I leave the command, I have time for two telephone calls. The first is to my mother. When she hears my voice, she is so excited. But as soon as she realises that I have come back because of the war, her maternal instinct takes over and she starts to yell at me: "Why did you come back? You should have waited for the army to call you!" After that, I call Shosh's parents. My father-in-law picks up, and he's surprised to hear me. He is very moved that I came back voluntarily: he is worried and tells me to be careful, but I can hear the pride in his voice that myself and others from the younger generation haven't left our parents to face the war alone.'

Shaul reaches the rest of his unit in El Arish on the third day of the war. As expected, nobody gives him a regulation weapon, so he faces his first mission with the .22 calibre rifle that he had bought in the States. 'Every so often, the Egyptians would shoot at us, but I didn't return fire, because my weapon was almost useless at any distance beyond 50–100 metres. It's not a pleasant feeling, being under enemy fire, but it's not the most dangerous situation I have ever been in. Crossing through a minefield is a far more nerve-racking experience than being under fire. A minefield is a completely different level of stress: you never know if you are taking the right step. You can only hope.

'We move from place to place with a jeep and a truck, and every time we find an abandoned position I dismantle a few parts from the cannons, turning them into useless lumps of metal, while we wait for another squad to follow us and take them back to the base. When we get back after sunset, I learn a valuable lesson about how the army attracts all kinds. Wearing a uniform doesn't make you a better person, much less some kind of hero. On the contrary, often those who pretend to be heroes are all talk, keeping themselves out of danger. They see war as just another path to personal gain, looking for a souvenir to take home with them. When they see the knife attached to my belt, a lot of people think I stole it from an Egyptian and ask me how they can also get one like it. I also discover that one of these "war heroes" has stolen the kitbag I had left behind with all my things in it. The following morning, we wake up and find that the truck we had loaded with the parts we removed from the Egyptian outposts had been emptied out overnight.'

On 10 June, the war ends. After less than a week, Israel now occupies three times the territory it held previously. Recounted in such brief words, it seems like an easy matter. It is not. Even though the shooting and bombing was brief, the number of dead and wounded is high. In six days, 759 Israelis and 15,000 Arabs have lost their lives.

Among the casualties on the first day is a US photographer, Paul Schutzer. Paul works for *Life* magazine, and he is good at his job: two years earlier, a photograph he takes sends shockwaves around the world. It's a close-up of a young Vietnamese man who is thought to be a member of the Viet Cong, blindfolded and with his mouth sealed with tape. His head is facing upwards, seeking mercy that may not come, his nostrils flared like those of a terrified animal condemned to the slaughter. *Life* deems the image worthy of the cover page of the issue published on 26 November 1965. The title above it reads: *The Blunt Reality of War in Vietnam*. The image rattles the conscience of the American people: war is not what they want you to think it is – war is deadly. Less than two years later, Paul himself is struck by a 57 mm projectile while sitting on top of an Israeli armoured personnel carrier. As with Robert Capa in Indochina before him, the roll of film that was inside his camera at the time is retrieved, developed and published posthumously. Those are the last images taken by Paul Schutzer. He was 36 years old when he died.

By 11 June, the ceasefire has already been signed. The situation does not change from one moment to the next for Shaul Ladany, whose work on the ground continues. For him, however, that date has a special significance, even before he is told that he will soon be returning home. 'I was supposed to be in Chicago on 11 June for the national championships over the Olympic distance of 50km. I had been training for an entire year without a break, thinking about this race that was supposed to send me to the Olympic Games in Mexico City. Before I left for Israel, I was in great form. I felt like I had a good chance of winning the race, and then I am dropped in the middle of the desert. Once the fighting is over, I try to train a bit at dawn, before leaving the base with my unit. It's not easy marching on the sandy ground, but that isn't what puts me off: there are charred corpses left on the ground everywhere, and the air is full of the terrible smell of decomposing remains.'

Two weeks later, his unit is dispersed and Shaul is granted permission to return to the USA. 'The kitbag that had been stolen from me also had my razor and shaving foam in it, so when I come back and my mother sees me, she finds herself staring at a newly bearded son. Like a lot of soldiers, I decide to keep it.' Before he returns to New York, Shaul goes to Jerusalem to see if their house has been struck in the Jordanian bombardment of the city. 'We are lucky: the house is OK, and a few days later I can hold Shosh once more. Even though she does not find my new "bearded veteran" look very attractive, she doesn't order me to shave it off, so the fur continues to grow on my face. At one stage, the beard has grown so long that during a race up and down the Coney Island boardwalk, every time I pass the start/finish line I hear people shouting: "The rabbi is coming, the rabbi is coming." They obviously don't know that I'm an atheist.' The racewalking, alongside the university studies, is the best way to process the experiences of war, to live with yet another gallery of horrors, injuries and mutilations. Back in the USA, Shaul is a veteran with no time for self-pity. There are no recurring nightmares filling his nights, only Olympic dreams. 'Before going back to the United States, I had spoken with Aharon Doron, the president of the Israeli Athletics Association: he told me that if I could improve my personal best time for the 50 km by around six minutes, I would be called up to the team for the Games.' With those words ringing in his ears, Shaul trained harder and more often than he had before the war.

After life in New York has returned to spinning on its regular axis, Shaul receives a letter: it is a reply from the head of the Artillery corps to the letter he had sent before the war broke out. In his reply, Colonel Israel Ben-Amitai thanks Shaul for his willingness to return to Israel to enlist in active service. He explains, however, that the speed with which the conflict has unfolded means that there is no need for him to return, and that the artillery batteries have successfully carried out their duties without having to inconvenience those living abroad. Mission accomplished. Shaul reads the letter, then puts it back in the envelope. And lets out a chuckle.

NINE

AN OLYMPIC PROFESSOR: MEXICO CITY 1968

'Let me see your documents.' The streets of California are so wide that even counting the number of lanes is a struggle. Vast freeways take their travellers wherever they need to go, provided they are sitting in a form of motorised transport. There is no space for pedestrians: walking along the freeway is a disruptive gesture, or at the very least that is how some perceive it. That is how Shaul finds himself standing in front of a police officer who wants to know why a man with a long beard and short shorts is walking among the Bay Area traffic. 'I had arrived at the airport and called my friend Billy Lopes, but he could not come and pick me up for at least three hours. So, I decided to make the most of the time: I changed in the bathroom at the terminal and left my luggage in a locker, and I started to racewalk, following directions I had been given at a petrol station. It was all going well until a police car pulled up next to me on my way back.'

It is the summer of 1968, and Shaul is training for his biggest goal, participating in the Olympic Games which are due to take place that October in Mexico City. The kilometres disappear behind him with a single thought occupying his mind and nothing that can stop him. Almost nothing.

'The policeman is standing in front of me, and our dialogue is almost surreal. "What are you doing?" he asks me.

'"Walking," I reply. It is very clear that my answer does not satisfy him, so he pushes further.

'"Why are you walking?"

'I don't want to waste any more time, so I spell out what seems to me to be clear and obvious: "I like walking and I'm training." Even this is not enough, and he wants to give me a fine, because I cannot be in the middle of the freeway and, mostly, because he thinks I'm a hippie who's mocking him. Luckily, I have my Columbia student card with me, and after a while I manage to convince him not to file a report. After that is agreed, I want to finish my training session, but there's no way: I am taken back to the airport in the backseat of his car, with a metal grille between me and this defender of the peace.'

It's not the first time that such an incident has befallen Shaul during a training session. A similar one occurred in New Jersey during an outdoor session with Elliott Denman and Don Johnson: a journalist, an engineer and an aspiring university lecturer, none wearing the typical clothes of their profession. Marathon running is not yet a popular sport (the first New York City Marathon will not take place until 1970, with only 127 participants) and grown men running through the streets is not a common sight. To make matters worse, they are not running, but racewalking, their swinging hips and unusual strides attracting curious stares. To protect himself from the cold, Elliott is wearing a pair of his wife's socks, while Shaul has on a pair of old and well-worn tracksuit trousers that are full of holes. Here too, their training session is interrupted by a policeman, and their enforced break ends only when the officer recognises Elliott as not a dangerous pervert, but rather as the respected columnist from the *Asbury Park Evening Press.*

Interruptions aside, from February 1968 onwards, Ladany is committed to the Olympic dream. He has organised his academic timetable so that his thesis is finished during the winter, leaving only the viva to tackle in the following months and a lot more time to dedicate to training. He also scales back his search for a position as a full professor: in the first semester of the 1967/68 academic year, he taught production management to first-year students at Columbia, but now he decides that his academic career can wait. Mexico City comes first. 'Until October, Shosh will be our only breadwinner, her scholarship our only source of income. I dedicate myself exclusively to training, twice a day, seven days a week. The benefits of this new fitness regime quickly become clear: in March I take part in a 50km track race, and, despite the rain, I complete it in 4 hours 29 minutes and 11 seconds. My fitness is so good that the day after the race I am able to complete an 80km training session.'

The amount of tarmac passing beneath Ladany's feet recalls a film that is in production at the same time by Sydney Pollack, with Jane Fonda in the starring role. It's called *They Shoot Horses, Don't They?* and it is not about racewalking, but about a dance marathon which continues uninterrupted for days at a time, the participants collapsing with exhaustion one after the other until only one couple is left standing. Will only one remain? Shaul has no time for questions. He has no time to dance and no time to go to the cinema. The only thought occupying his mind is to rack up the kilometres, so many that he could reach Mexico City without taking a single flight: there are 4,200 of them from New York, a distance that Ladany – with his new, relentless self-imposed training regime – covers in just over two months. And it's not only a question of quantity, but also of quality. The Olympics are not a pleasant summer afternoon stroll; there are times that must be met in order to qualify. The Games are a celebration that is open to many, but not to all; a highly selective party with an entrance ticket which cannot be bought. It can only be earned, with sweat and pain which accompanies you to bed at the end of the day when it's time to sleep. Shaul knows that, if he wants to be part of the Israeli team, he has to be able to maintain a pace of 5 minutes and 16 seconds per kilometre over a distance of 50km. This means an average of just under 12km an hour; it may seem easy – it is not. Many people would struggle to keep up that sort of pace while running. Ladany must do it racewalking. His legs become a compass with which to map out the world, one piece at a time. The final stretch is in San Francisco, within the Golden Gate

Park, the location of the 1968 US Championships. Here, in the shadow of the famous red bridge, Shaul earns his place in the delegation by completing the race in 4 hours and 23 minutes, below the target time set by the Israeli Athletics Association. The Games are afoot.

Now the preparation begins. Getting to the Olympics is an achievement in itself, but only up to a point. To do things properly, Ladany joins the US team, who have organised a high-altitude training camp by Lake Tahoe in the Sierra Nevada to prepare for the altitude of Mexico City. The US athletes are accommodated in a facility set up for the occasion, where Shaul is hosted for a few days while he makes his own arrangements. He leaves a series of notes on the message boards of the shops in the town, and his call is answered by a couple who show up in a white Corvette. Their names are Donna Pritchett and Warren Harding: Shaul doesn't know them, but Warren – a 44-year-old athlete – is something of a celebrity in climbing circles. In 1958, he led the first expedition to reach the summit of El Capitan, in Yosemite National Park, and he was known to his fellow climbers as 'Batso' for his ability to sleep while hanging from walls using equipment that he himself had designed and created, with Donna's assistance. They read Shaul's notice and are willing to help him, offering him a place in their bungalow. 'Deep down, I think they think I'm a bit crazy, seeing me doing almost 80km every day. On the other hand, they enjoy climbing and hanging on to bits of rock. The way I see it, everyone is a little bit crazy in their own way.'

Crazy, friendly and willing to help. The small bungalow even has space for Shoshana, who leaves New York to be with her husband, having packed up all the possessions they have accumulated over three years of life in the USA. To help them move, the Ladanys have a Volkswagen Beetle given to them by Ron Laird – a racewalker with Team USA – in exchange for a promise to drive it down to Los Angeles before the start of the Games. A place to sleep, a car for transport: Shaul and his friends may not be flower children, but they know the value of sharing. 'With Ron's Beetle, we move to Yosemite Park, where Donna works, so that Shosh can do some sightseeing and I can keep training around the trails in the park. I cover dozens of kilometres all by myself, in the middle of nature. A wonderful sight, although I have to keep reminding myself to keep my eyes open: at Lake Tahoe I found myself face to face with a herd of deer, but more than that, I remember once seeing a rattlesnake pursuing a mouse. In Yosemite, nothing happens to me during the practice walks, but we do have a close encounter on the first night, when we stop in an area set up for people to sleep in sleeping bags. Donna has warned us that there are a lot of grizzly bears around, so we pitch our camp a long way from the tables and make sure there is no food nearby. We must have missed something, though: in the middle of the night a pack of bears wakes us up. They are fighting over an empty tin, and we can hear the sound of their teeth sinking into the metal. We stay very still, paralysed inside our sleeping bags, careful not to make any sound that might attract their attention. And we wait for the dawn.' Despite the bears, that night is not the most exhausting experience Shaul has to contend with before the Olympics. That is an honour reserved for Mexican bureaucracy.

As soon as he successfully meets the Olympic target time, Ladany applies for the special entrance visa for athletes. He has not yet received instructions from the Israeli committee, however, so he decides to show up at the Mexican consulate in Los Angeles. 'I want to speed up the whole process, so that I can cross the border as soon as possible and give myself time to adjust to the altitude, which everyone is saying will be one of the biggest challenges in the endurance races. I'm outside the consulate first thing in the morning, with a letter in my hand that confirms my status as part of an Olympic team. When I explain my request to one of the staff members, his response is blunt: "The Vice-Consul is examining visa requests at the moment."

'I have no choice, I wait. I'm there for the whole day inside those offices, watching as the clock ticks, until finally – late in the afternoon – my name is called. A junior member of staff explains that he cannot provide me with the document because the Foreign Ministry has already issued a special visa for athletes participating in the Games, and everything has already been sent to the national Olympic committees. The explanation is straightforward, but I have not been sent anything from Israel, and obviously I will not be coming with the rest of the squad from Tel Aviv, seeing as I am currently 200 km from the Mexican border. At this point, the easiest solution would be to get a tourist visa. However, he explains to me, that means filling out another request, which can only be submitted the next day.'

The door seems open from here. Shoshana had no

trouble getting her own tourist visa, and there is no reason to think that things should be dragged out. There is no sensible reason for a simple piece of paper to turn into a diplomatic incident. However, the response on the second day remains negative: it is not possible to provide a tourist visa to an athlete who is entitled to an Olympic visa. On the third day, before returning to the Mexican consulate, Ladany turns to the Israeli consulate first to ask for support. This time, in addition to the invitation letter, he has another one that reiterates and confirms all the requirements. Enough? No, because it's Friday afternoon and the Vice-Consul is busy. Come back on Monday.

After the weekend, Shaul decides to call on a higher power: he asks the Israeli Consul himself to intervene on his behalf with his Mexican counterpart, and this time his visa request comes with three letters. Despite this, the fourth day also comes and goes without a reply. 'By the fifth day, I know my way around the offices of the Mexican consulate off by heart. I'm more and more exasperated, because I'm losing so much precious training time, and being sent from one desk to another is draining my energy. I wonder whether this delay has been created to make me pay some kind of bribe, but I have never given or taken a bribe in my life, and I definitely don't plan to start now. By the afternoon, my patience has run out: I start to raise my voice and to threaten them with a press conference where I will say that they are trying to prevent an athlete from participating in the Olympic Games. The next day, before I go back to the consulate for the sixth time in eight days. I send a telegram to the Israeli embassy in Mexico City, warning them that I will be coming whether I have a visa or not, even if I get myself arrested in the process. It's a miracle: the precious visa is given to me on the same day.' Now Shaul Ladany has everything he needs to participate in the Olympic Games.

Altitude is not the only problem in Mexico City. On 2 October, a few days before the Games are due to begin, a peaceful student-led protest in the Plaza de las Tres Culturas turns into a bloodbath when the army and police open fire on the protesters. The massacre is witnessed by Oriana Fallaci, who is present in the square and gets shot in the back and leg. 'It was worse than Vietnam,' the journalist will later write in *L'Europeo* magazine. 'In Vietnam, when you're in the middle of a battle, you try to protect yourself, to save yourself, you throw yourself into a hole in the ground, you throw yourself into a bunker, you take shelter behind anything you find and while you do that there's no police officer with his pistol drawn trying to stop you.' The number of victims is never precisely established – some speak of dozens, others of hundreds of fatalities. What is not in doubt, however, is that army trucks surrounded the square while helicopters flew overhead and fired flares, as soldiers advanced and began firing into the crowds.

The massacre does not halt the Olympics. Ten days later, the Games begin as planned, and on 16 October there is already a new story to fill front pages around the world: during the medal ceremony of the 200 m event, Tommie Smith and John Carlos receive the American anthem with bowed heads, no shoes and closed fists raised to the sky. The anti-segregationist protest has reached the podium, and the President of the IOC – the same Avery Brundage who, four years later, will wash his hands of the bloodshed in Munich with a few cursory words – is outraged by what he considers an intolerable provocation, an affront. One gesture is not like another: as the head of the US delegation at the 1936 Berlin Olympics, Brundage had not raised any objections when athletes turned towards the crowd with their arms raised in a Nazi salute.

The times are changing, and black Americans are not the only ones stealing the show: for the first time at the Games, all the distance running events – from the 800m to the marathon – are won by athletes from Africa. This is only one of the reasons why the Mexico City Games goes down in history: it is the occasion on which East Germany makes its debut; a malformed and pharmacologically assisted utopia that is fated to disappear after taking 309 medals in five Olympic Games. It is 22-year-old Bob Beamon's leap into infinity, soaring so far in the long jump that the distance is incalculable at first for a young man used to thinking in feet and inches. It is the introduction of anti-doping measures, with pentathlete Hans-Gunnar Liljenwall the first to be singled out after drinking two beers; something which will doubtless raise a grin on the faces of future generations who grow up on a diet of bread and clenbuterol. The decision creates an equivalence between Liljenwall and the East Germans, even though the poor Swede – stripped of his bronze medal for excessive alcohol consumption – defends himself by arguing that he had drunk a bit too much in order to calm his nerves ahead of the shooting event.

Shaul does not see all these events as part of a historical context – for him it is the daily routine of life in the Olympic Village alongside people like Abebe Bikila. The Ethiopian champion, now no longer barefoot, had dominated the marathon event in Rome 1960 and Tokyo 1964, and his two Olympic gold medals make him one of the most renowned athletes in the world, owing to the exposure from the global broadcast of the Games. From close up, however, he does not seem overly friendly. Not to Ladany, anyway. 'After meeting him, I was left with the impression of someone quite dull. I get on better with the Tunisian athlete Mohammed Gammoudi, who, aside from anything else, is the only athlete from an Arab country I am able to speak with. The others cut the conversation short the moment I say I am Israeli. I enjoy the spirit inside the Olympic Village, though. Because I speak eight languages, I can say something to everyone, and people will often come looking for "the Israeli with the beard" to use me as an interpreter. Every so often Shosh also joins me, because entering the village is anything but difficult. She can wear my tracksuit top and it is enough.' Security is not a priority. It will only become one after Munich.

Shaul prepares for his race, while his relationship with the heads of the Israeli delegation is becoming increasingly strained. The visa issue was only the start: nobody has bothered to provide Ladany with an official uniform, so for the opening ceremony he must take the initiative himself and seek out a Mexican tailor. Another clash comes during a public engagement with the Jewish community of Mexico. As the evening drags on and on, Shaul insists that the athletes be allowed to return to the village to rest. Permission denied and another admonishment. So it continues, until a few days before the 50 km event, when not only does Ladany have no official member of the delegation to support him by passing bottles of water at the refreshment stations, but he does not even have a Team Israel shirt to use in the race. He decides to improvise. He is accustomed to relying on the kindness of strangers, and this time is no different. Together with Shosh, Shaul pins notes asking for support in Hebrew around local hotels and at the entrances to the Olympic Village. Help comes from Maya and Yossi Ramon, a couple from Eilat on holiday in Mexico, and an Israeli journalist who wants to film the event and offers his car. Now all that's left is to find a kit for the race, but here an easy, hand-crafted solution presents itself: with a blue ballpoint pen, Ladany painstakingly writes ISRAEL across the front and back of a white shirt. From a distance, the result appears immaculate. During the race, however, sweat and spillage from his refreshments mix with ink, and by the finish line the effect is a psychedelic pattern resembling a Rorschach inkblot. Hardly in keeping with the branded uniforms that are gaining dominance during those years, with seemingly everyone sporting Adidas stripes or leaping pumas.

It is not the lack of a symbol that holds him back in the race, but the necessary support. Shosh and the three volunteers they have recruited do their best, but without a pass, they are held back by the police and unable to reach all the refreshment stations along the way. In order to avoid dehydration, Shaul is forced to top up the Coca-Cola mixed with glucose that his body is best equipped to digest with water from the sponges that are passed to him along the way and the orange juice which he picks up from the tables. The effect starts to make itself felt at around the 35th kilometre, when not only his legs are on the move, but also his bowels. 'Eventually I cannot fight it any more. I leave the track, crouch behind a hedge and answer the call of nature. While I am crouched there, a Mexican spectator, taking pity on me, passes me a newspaper. It's clear to both of us that he doesn't think I need the reading material.' Despite the unintended break, which sees him slip outside the top 20, Ladany is able to continue the race, and in the last few kilometres he finds himself shoulder to shoulder with a Mexican rival, Pablo Colin. 'The crowd goes crazy. They're shouting "Pablo, Pablo" louder and louder, as we get closer and closer to the finish line. Every time I try to overtake him, a scooter moves in front of me, and I must breathe in its exhaust fumes while the police do nothing. I only break free when we are about to enter the stadium, when finally, I can overtake. I finish 24th, in a time of 5 hours 1 minute and 6 seconds. Colin crosses the line 24 seconds later.' The winner is Christoph Höhne from East Germany, and his time is a testament to the difficulty of racewalking at an altitude of over 2,000m: his winning time, 4 hours 20 minutes and 13 seconds, is slower than Ladany's best time, set at sea level. It is almost ten minutes off the winning pace in Tokyo four years previously, and almost 25 minutes slower than Munich four years later. Among those who pay the price are the outgoing champion, Abdon Pamich from Italy, and the Englishman Paul Nihill (silver medallist in Tokyo 1964), both of whom are forced to retire. Two British athletes cross the finish line: Bryan Eley, seventh in a time of 4 hours 37 minutes and 32 seconds; and Shaun Lightman, 18th in a time of 4 hours 52 minutes and 20 seconds.

With that result, Ladany's Olympics are over and he can finally rest after months of gruelling training that have brought his weight down to 62 kg, eight less than he would usually weigh. His first action is a symbolic one; the day after the race, the beard is shaved off. 'Then Shosh and I decide to do some sightseeing in Mexico. We go by bus, and that is an experience in itself, because we share the trip with chickens and other animals that the farmers load alongside the luggage. The thing that really amazes us, though, is a stop in the middle of the jungle. A farmer at the side of the road waves his hand, and the driver stops to pick him up. First, though, the man has to go and get something: he dives into the vegetation and comes back with a rope in his hand, with an enormous boar attached to the other end that he loads into the luggage compartment before calmly climbing on board. Shosh and I stare the whole time. But we are the only ones surprised by what we have just seen.

'The Mayan ruins at Chichén Itzá and Uxmal, in the state of Yucatán, are incredible, although we have an unpleasant experience there: I have my tracksuit top on, with *ISRAEL* stamped across the shoulders, and as I pass by two men, I hear one of them say to the other '*schwein*' – 'pig' in German.

'That word alone is enough to make me explode: I turn around, grab him by the arm, and, speaking English, ask him to repeat what he's just said.

'In a strong German accent, he mutters: "I didn't say anything."

'I want to beat him, but I restrain myself.'

The episode does not spoil the memory of the Games. The Ladanys are able to return to Mexico City in time for the closing ceremony, and Shaul is in the middle of the Olympic Stadium as thousands of doves are released and take to the skies. 'An unforgettable moment . . . and some of them decide to leave another little souvenir for us as they go. One of which lands right on my head.'

TEN

A SOUVENIR OF DEATH

From the Olympic track to a university lecture hall, perspectives change quickly. All in the time it takes to fly back to Israel. On his return, Shaul sets aside his training routine for a while: not a decision, a necessity. Tel Aviv University has hired him to teach at the Graduate School of Business Administration, and the early days are tough. 'The impact of it almost overwhelms me: I have been asked to teach six different courses, and because I do not have any existing materials to rely on, my days start at sunrise and end late at night. When I am not with the students, I am surrounded by books and notes for my classes. The lack of kilometres begins to take its toll. I've gone from full steam ahead to almost nothing; everything hurts, I struggle to sleep at night, and Shosh says I have become irritable and difficult to be around.'

As the months go by, life returns to its course and Shaul's twin spirits – the professor and the racewalker – can find harmony and balance; he even begins to race again. And to win. The results of the previous years and the media coverage that followed have given him a measure of popularity, but the most meaningful sign of his success is when he begins to appear in crosswords: *Successful participant in the Galilee racewalking event, the Mt Tabor Race and the Yehiam March, all on the same day, 6 letters?* Ladany. *Winner of the first 100 km racewalk in Israel in May 1969, 6 letters?* The same: Ladany. *The winner of two gold medals, in the 3 km and 10 km events, at the Maccabiah Games?* Him again: Ladany.

'My name is well known, but my face is not so much, which leads to humorous situations. The funniest is when I am in a military outpost during the War of Attrition, the war between Israel and Egypt from 1967 to 1970. I have been asked to give a talk to the soldiers deployed along the Bar-Lev Line, along the eastern banks of the Suez Canal. At dawn, before the meeting, I decide to do some training inside the base, and a few times I cross paths with the occupants there.

'One of them shouts from behind me: "You have no chance. Ladany is better!"

'Another is more encouraging and tells me: "Perhaps one day you could even beat Ladany."

'I carry on, smiling. When I am taken inside the bunker where the lesson is supposed to take place, a few of the people recognise me, and the subject of my talk is changed on the spot. I was supposed to speak about the use of quantitative tools in management, but everybody prefers to hear anecdotes from the Olympic Games instead. It's a triumph. I remain at the front for two days, escorted from one outpost to another. There are frequent attacks, and along the road are warning signs like the one we see across from Ismailia, which reads: "This area is exposed to the Egyptian side. During bombardments, cross quickly."

'Luckily, on those two days, everything is quiet. The only small incident takes place when they take me to sleep away from the frontlines, around 20 km back. It's a form of mobile base for the tank platoons which changes location every night to make it harder to pinpoint and attack. After we arrive, I decide to stretch my legs in the area: the sun has just set, I'm in the middle of nowhere and the only sound is the breeze. Suddenly, when I'm a few kilometres from the camp, I hear a jeep approaching. Inside it is the commander's assistant, who pulls up next to me and orders me to get into the vehicle immediately. He calls me crazy: apparently Egyptian commando forces often cross the border in this area.'

Ladany would have made a valuable hostage to parade if captured. He is not a regular soldier – he is sent to the front to keep the morale of the troops high by regaling them with stories of his Olympic adventures. His achievements have afforded him such a reputation that at the closing ceremony of the 1969 Maccabiah Games, he is chosen to lower the flag, while a 19-year-old swimmer from California stands next to him as a guard of honour. The young American by his side is not some wet-behind-the-ears student: the boy has returned from the Mexico City Olympic Games the year before with four medals, but he is not satisfied. His name is Mark Spitz, and he is training to achieve what no man has ever achieved before. And he does: four years later, in Munich, he will take home seven gold medals to show off alongside his beaming moustachioed grin.

Shaul is already 33 years old and cannot allow himself to focus exclusively on training. Alongside his academic commitments, there are also his reserve duties, because military life in Israel continues long after the mandatory period of national service, and every so often he gets called up. 'In the space of 12 months, between 1969 and 1970, I spend almost a hundred days in uniform. Military service affects everyone at the university to some degree, students and younger professors. We try to arrange it so that the courses can continue as much as possible: I do it by doubling my lectures when I am not in the army, and entrusting them to my assistants when I am.' The War of Attrition is less intense than the Six Day War, but it is still no game. Provocations and skirmishes along the new borders often escalate into full-scale artillery warfare.

'In November 1969, I am assigned to a regiment in the north-east, in the Beit She'an Valley. I am essentially given command of one of the three artillery batteries in the regiment, which is equipped with Russian 122mm cannons seized during the Six Day War. Our mission is to provide cover fire for the troops or to strike targets provided to us by the Intelligence units. One day, we are deployed to a trench on a crest to the east of Kibbutz Hamadia, when we are given the order to fire. This lasts for two or three minutes, and based on our experience, we know that the Jordanians need five minutes to identify the location of the fire, aim their cannons and respond. I order all my men to take cover in the fortified bunkers that can withstand even a direct hit. I stay in the command post along with a technician and Staff Sergeant Shmuel Miller, and a few minutes later I receive a call on the telephone giving me permission to send the technician to the bunker, too. I don't need to say a word: a nod is enough for him to start running towards the entrance to the structure. Shmuel and I are told to stay where we are with the field telephone, because the bunker can only be reached by the main line. The enemy fire begins. We hear the return fire landing close by, while we stay in our trench, which is about a metre-and-a-half deep. Finally, the call arrives, authorising us to go to the bunker. I yell to Shmuel: "Run!" and I follow him, with explosions all around us. Some of the missiles explode before they even hit the ground. I run as fast as possible: I have never gone so fast in my life and now I can see the entrance to the bunker in front of me. A few more metres and I will be safe. I enter the bunker horizontally, half-diving and half-falling in. Right behind me, I hear a huge crash. It's not incoming fire, it is Shmuel, who could not keep up with me over the distance and now lands on top of me. We are alive. I regret that nobody timed me, because I would have set a new world record over 100 m.

'When I return home after my service is complete, I take a souvenir with me – a fragment of a missile which I picked up next to our post. I show it to Shosh and tell her: "This missed me." A shard of metal that bears the signs of the explosion and reminds Ladany that, once again, he was lucky. Being alive and well means reclaiming his daily routine, day by day, which for Shaul means racewalking and university. Training and lectures, races and exams: lining them up, one after the other, his days fill up and it is as if Ladany has flicked a switch. On the one hand is the professor and racewalker, on the other is the soldier. If you want to avoid coming under siege from your emotions, you have to be able to control them, and Shaul has been doing that since childhood. He was young when he first learned not to cry, and he has remained steadfast ever since. Even when he comes home from war.

ELEVEN

TO THE SOUNDS OF BIG BEN

Surviving alone is not enough. Shaul wants to squeeze out everything he can from every single day. Twenty-four hours, 1,440 minutes; each and every movement is meticulously calibrated and optimised to allow the many pieces of his life to fit into place.

'Like all young couples, Shoshana and I dream of buying a house. To make it possible, I take on consulting work along with my university job and accept the various offers I receive. I teach individual courses at other institutions, from engineering management to quality control, and do research for the Bank of Israel and for the Ministry of Commerce and Industry. This means that I do not have a minute to spare. I have come up with a few tricks to help me fit everything in. Take meals, for example: when

I leave the house in the morning, I take a container with my food with me, and I eat on the journey from one college to another. When I get into the car, I tuck a large napkin into the collar of my shirt and put the container on my lap, and at every traffic light I put a forkful of food in my mouth. My bag with my training kit is always in the boot, and the car is also my changing room, so I don't waste a single minute.'

At the start of 1970, Ladany is back in shape and decides that Mexico City was not enough. Even though he is now 34, he intends to return for another Olympic Games. He makes the most of the spring break from classes to take part in a series of competitions in the United States and Europe, to put his ambitions to the test. He is better prepared than he was in the past – not only in terms of his training regime, but also in terms of his equipment for races. 'I now always have a large sponge and a one-litre thermos flask with a spout designed to make drinking easier. It's an array that raises eyebrows when I come to the airport. There have been attacks and hijackings on airplanes in recent months, so my luggage inspection starts to become particularly thorough.'

Explosive threats? Only the muscles in Ladany's legs, which carry him to the finish line of a 50-mile track race in a new record time (7 hours 52 minutes). The day after that effort, Shaul is back on board a plane, this time heading to a race in Lausanne, Switzerland. 'That race is only 25km, but I'm still a bit tired from the effort of the track race in New Jersey. At the end of the competition, I talk to one of the coaches of the East German delegation and I find out from him that a lot of the German athletes are going on to a race in Sesto San Giovanni, near Milan. It is not included in my plans, but I decide to follow them, and board the first train to Italy.'

Here, Ladany's career meets the most important racewalking event in Italy. Sesto is known as the 'Stalingrad of Italy', partly because of the city's fierce resistance to the Nazi-Fascist occupation and partly for the Tito-esque majority which the Partito Comunista Italiano (Italian Communist Party) receives at every election. A working-class city that decided to celebrate the annual International Workers' Day by inviting racewalkers to toil through the streets. The race was established in 1957 – five years after Pino Dordoni's Olympic triumph in Helsinki – and it quickly became a regular fixture on the international circuit.

'It is basically a replica of the Olympic Games. Everyone is there: Russians, Germans, Poles,

Hungarians, Czechoslovakians . . . my train from Switzerland arrives at 11 a.m. and the race is due to start at 2 p.m.; I just about have time to prepare myself for the start.'

One of those who remember Ladany's preparations is Daniele Redaelli, not yet 18 years old at the time and already a contributor to the local newspaper, *Luce Sestese*. Redaelli would go on to serve as the editor-in-chief of the *Gazzetta dello Sport*, the most widely read Italian daily newspaper: 'I'm observing Ladany as he gets changed, when he comes over to me and asks to borrow a pen. I pass it to him and watch as he writes *ISRAEL* on his shirt in block letters.' Two years have passed since the Mexico City Games, yet the kit situation still leaves something to be desired. This time, the effect is like a tattoo. 'When I see him again at the end of the race,' says Redaelli, 'the ink has soaked into his skin through the shirt. Now the text in blue, *ISRAEL*, is written across his chest.' The race is a baptism for Ladany; his first competition in Italy. It is a debut that leaves him enchanted. 'They say it's 30km, but in the end it turns out to be closer to 32km. Either way, it is a bit short for my taste. But it is worth it just for the crowd: I have never experienced enthusiasm like it. There are people on both sides of the street, and they cheer on everybody, not only the Italians. At around halfway, it starts to rain, and I expect the crowd to go home, but I have underestimated them. They open their umbrellas and cover themselves with those plastic sheets as well as they can. And continue to cheer even when the rain begins to pour down.'

Among those cheering Shaul on is a young boy, 8 years old, called Raffaello Ducceschi. He lives in Sesto and has watched the racewalkers arrive on 1 May from around the world every year since he can remember. In the 1980s, Ducceschi will go on to win the competition himself and become the most successful 50 km racewalking Italian of his age, qualifying for two Olympic Games, taking fifth place in Los Angeles 1984 and eighth in Seoul 1988. Raffaello attaches himself to Shaul and does not let him out of his sight. He follows him, metre after metre, all the while preserving images that would remain ingrained in his memory like a Polaroid film. 'If you support them during the race on your bike, you're in the middle of it too. On the pavement you're far away. But on your bike! You can hear their breathing, feel their sweat,' he will later write in the book *Sesto San Giovanni, una città in marcia*. 'I chose someone who nobody else was supporting. One who was not going to win. Bald head, round glasses, skinny, like all the racewalkers, a white shirt with *ISRAEL* written on it in blue . . . I tried to bring him something to drink; "Give him some water" someone shouted at me from the crowd. And I obeyed. I went into a café and got them to bring me a bottle. But he didn't want the water. Doesn't drink. He is my hero. I don't care if he wins or not. He reminds me of a drawing I have seen, a portrait of Father Kolbe – a Catholic priest who was martyred at Auschwitz. Perhaps the incongruity escaped me. But I was so close. As a child he had been miraculously saved at the Bergen-Belsen concentration camp.'

Shaul finishes the race in 13th place, satisfied. He then tries to sign up for another classic event, Prague to Poděbrady, but diplomatic relations between Israel and the countries of the Warsaw Pact have been broken off in the wake of the Six Day War, and obtaining a visa proves impossible.

During the summer, Ladany goes back to teaching in the United States for three months, at Rutgers University in New Jersey, renting a house a few blocks away from where he had lived during his Columbia days. That is when he decides to prepare for the London to Brighton, an 85km event. 'The United Kingdom is the birthplace of racewalking, and everyone tells me that this event, which started in the 19th century, is the most prestigious race in the country. The idea of trying to win it is tempting, and I spend the whole summer training with it in my mind. It's not easy though, because all the way until the day I leave I am busy with a research project which will later be published in *Management Science*.'

Professor Ladany goes to London, but not much remains of the Swinging Sixties: The Beatles have released *Let It Be* and are on the verge of splitting up, and a few weeks before Ladany's arrival a new minister had been appointed to lead the Department of Education – a 44-year-old Conservative politician by the name of Margaret Thatcher.

The journey from the United States to Europe is in the finest Ladany tradition: Shaul leaves the university and takes a taxi to pick up Shosh at the last minute. She is waiting for him at home, the suitcases packed, and from there they go straight to the airport to board a night flight to London. They land in the capital on Friday afternoon, less than 20 hours before the start of the race. 'The organisers have arranged for us to sleep in a YMCA in Stockwell, in south London. When we get to the hostel, my arms are aching after carrying the suitcases, which are very heavy after we crammed three months' worth of life in New York into them. I spend the remaining hours arranging ice packs for my refreshment during the race, and contacting Shmuel Benkler, who is to be my support. At 4.30 a.m., he and his son come and pick me up to take me to the starting point: the race is due to start at 6 a.m. from Parliament Square, and when it comes, I am taken by surprise. I have never taken part in a race before where a bell is used to send people on their way, and here it is not just any bell – it's Big Ben. While I stand there and listen to it chiming 6 o'clock, the others are already a few metres ahead and moving. No problem: in almost no time I am up with the leading group, and with 15km behind me I already have an advantage of 50m or so. The organisers think I am gambling, that I have started off too strong, and they bet I won't even make it to the 50th kilometre. My support team do a wonderful job with the refreshments: Shmuel parks the car, stands at the side of the road and yells what I want to drink to Shosh, who is standing about 50m further along the road and has time to prepare it. Shmuel's son stands a bit further on with a sponge immersed in a bucket of ice water. Thanks to them, I have everything I need.

'At the halfway point, however, I take a wrong turn at a roundabout. By the time I hear people shouting to warn me about the mistake, Ray Middleton, my closest rival, is already ahead of me. When I reach him, we match each other, pace for pace, for almost 20km. I really need to pee, but I try to resist, because every second counts in these situations. Ray must have the same problem . . . at a certain point he cannot contain it any longer and he stops. I make the most of those few seconds to make a break. We are at Dale Hill, the most challenging climb of the course, and I am still in front. There are just over 10km left, and I am now more than 400m ahead of my nearest rival, but I cannot relax and every so often I ask Shmuel and Shosh whether there is anyone gaining ground on me. It is very hot, and I am afraid of being caught, so I keep pushing ahead like a madman. My racing strategy is very simple and has always been the same, especially when there is an uphill section involved: in the flat sections I go all-out, squeezing every last bit of energy out of myself until there is nothing left and I am unable to accelerate even a tiny bit. And then, when I reach an uphill section, I push even harder. Some might disagree with it, but that's my way. And here in Brighton it works perfectly: we are finally into the city and there are police officers stopping the traffic to let me pass. I see the finish line. I reach it. I've won.'

Ladany completes the course in 7 hours 46 minutes and 37 seconds. Only two people – Olympic gold medallists Abdon Pamich (Tokyo 1964) and Don Thompson (Rome 1960) – have ever gone faster in the history of the London to Brighton.

The prize for the winner is a relaxing session at the Brighton spa: exclusive access for a warm soak in the premier bath in the complex. 'Shosh complains that I was the first one in and the last one out. I say that, now that the race is over, I have no more reason to be in a hurry.' Immersed in the water, Shaul can let go of the minutes as they pass. No timing and no training to squeeze in among a thousand other commitments: after 85 km, the only thought is to enjoy the victory. A ritual that will repeat itself in 1971 and 1973. For Shaul Ladany, Brighton is a paradise.

TWELVE

MUNICH 1972: DACHAU, THE RACE, AND THE FINAL HOURS TOGETHER

The flight is delayed, and Shaul is more impatient than he has ever been. Showing up late for a race is a recurring nightmare for any athlete, but this is something worse. How do you explain to your daughter that her father wasn't there at her birth? How do you tell her that *Aba* (Dad) had been busy walking abroad? Better for the airport staff in Brussels to resolve the problem and fast, otherwise they won't be the ones to face the consequences. It will be you, the absent father without a particularly convincing explanation.

It is the summer of 1971 and the Ladany family is expanding: the date for Shosh's caesarean delivery has been known some time in advance, and in early July, Shaul leaves for Belgium confident that he will be back in time for the birth of Danit. He takes part in the Belgian national championships over 50 km in Charleroi and wins. Without the push of his US counterparts, competing in Europe is the only way to ensure adequate competition and the right conditions to continue to be competitive on an international stage: in Israel there is no suitable competition, and the summer heat makes even training a challenge. Luckily, the technical issues in Brussels are resolved in time, and when Danit emerges, her father is there to welcome her.

Two weeks later, however, he has to bid her farewell once again: there is the Hastings to Brighton to attend and the diary for September is also full of appointments. There is only a year to go before the Munich Olympics, and Shaul is sacrificing everything to be there at the Olympiastadion when the final torchbearer enters the stadium and the Games get under way. 'The Athletics Committee has selected four Olympic hopefuls and has decided to send them to Europe to train and compete. I am one of the four, but I decide that I cannot be away for almost two months in a row while Danit is still so young, so I make different arrangements. I leave with the others, then come back to my daughter for three weeks, then go back to Europe for two more races.' Balancing being an athlete and a father is not easy. There are those who move into another room when the baby is young to avoid losing hours of sleep. There are others who barely manage to attend the birth between trips and meetings. And there is Shaul who, as with his academic career, attempts to balance all his commitments. Albeit for the first few months, Danit always sees him with a suitcase in his hand.

The tour de force begins with another victory at the Hastings to Brighton, after which Ladany returns to Israel, subjecting himself once more to a gruelling training routine that does not leave much time for family life.

Once he has a goal in mind, Shaul does not go in for half measures. 'In addition to the daily sessions, on Fridays I do a longer trip, pushing myself as far as 100km. The temperature in Israel in August can go above 40 ºC, so to avoid the worst of the heat, I leave home at 3 o'clock in the morning. That is how I prepare for my encore at the London to Brighton event.'

He is rewarded for his many sacrifices with the congratulations of the Mayor of Brighton as he hands Ladany the winner's trophy for the second year in a row.

Sometimes, however, a lot is not enough, as Shaul finds out when the Israeli newspapers criticise him – a few days after his success in the UK – for retiring part way through a 50km event in Munich which has been put on as a test event for the Olympics. Shaul ends the race on a stretcher, exhausted from a bout of the flu before the race, but even the sirens of the ambulance are not enough to silence the critics. Nor is third place at the classic 100km event in Lugano – one of the most famous events in the world, where he is beaten only by the Olympic gold medallist from Mexico City, Höhne, and his East German counterpart, Selzer – sufficient to spare him the slings and arrows. It is made worse by the ongoing tensions in his relationship with the Israeli sporting establishment. Used to dealing with emerging athletes in their early 20s, they are ill-equipped for one who is as demanding as he is diligent. Ladany is not a child who can be deceived with long-winded, empty speeches. At 35 years old, he is a professor with a successful academic career, and a soldier who has fought in two wars. He is not the type to be intimidated by arrogant suits with honorary titles and a habit of raising their voices.

Every trip or request for technical support becomes

an arm wrestle. If he is to make it to the Munich Games, Professor Ladany will have to earn his place the hard way.

With that in mind, over the following months Shaul self-imposes a training and lifestyle regime that is even more rigorous than the ones before. 'I reach an agreement with the university to double my load for the first semester, to keep the entire second semester free. For the second part of my academic year, I will focus only on my research and the graduate students I am supervising. For the rest of the time, I am free to racewalk.' He creates a Herculean training schedule for himself that demands 350–430km every week. During the months when he is teaching, he leaves home at 3.30 a.m., starting the day with 50km and arriving just in time for class.

Thanks to this regime (or perhaps, in view of less punishing approaches which have gained traction in the years since, it might be argued that *despite* this regime), the results begin to arrive: Ladany clears the Olympic target time, improving his personal best in Charleroi over 50km, setting a time of 4 hours 17 minutes and 3 seconds. He follows that up with another notable achievement, breaking the world record for 50 miles with 200 laps of the track in Ocean

Township, New Jersey – completing the distance in 7 hours 23 minutes and 50 seconds.

When going round in circles, however, it is easy to lose track of your surroundings and your points of reference. 'While in the United States, I receive a telegram from Shosh. It says "*Mazal tov!* I am able to sit. Danit." I am so self-absorbed at the time that it takes me a while to understand that the congratulations are not for me, but for my daughter who, at the age of nine months, has learned to sit.'

When Shaul returns home after another of the countless races and training programmes abroad, little Danit struggles to recognise her father. United States, Germany, Italy, Switzerland ... time to unpack, repack and go again. United Kingdom, Denmark, Switzerland again, Greece, another short break at home and away once more. Belgium, Switzerland for a third time, France and the Netherlands. In four months between April and July 1972, the journey to the Olympics for Shaul adds dozens of stamps to his passport, collected from one airport to the next.

'It was understood that, for an Israeli during that period, flying was a risk. Hijackings, bombs on board, attacks at airports: I knew all of it, but I never thought about not going, not even once. More than once, I took off from or landed at an airport where an attack had taken place not long before. Or flew with an airline which had been targeted by a terrorist attack.' Rome, Zurich, Athens, West Berlin, Brussels: starting in the late 1960s, the list grows long. More often than not, the airline in the crosshairs is El Al, the Israeli national carrier, but it is not the only one. And the terrorists even manage to strike at the heart of Israel, inside the airport in Tel Aviv: on 30 May 1972, 28 people are killed and 80 are wounded after three members of the Japanese Red Army – a terrorist group with close ties to the Popular Front for the Liberation of Palestine – open fire within the terminal and in the landing area.

There are only a few weeks to go before the Olympic Games, and as Munich draws closer, the risks increase. The Israeli delegation is considered a target, but the security measures – such as they are – appear inadequate from the beginning. Germany is eager to erase the militaristic memories of the Berlin Olympic Games in 1936, and so the only security within the village consists of unarmed agents and security officials wearing uniforms in pastel hues. Their only contribution – in the most generous interpretation – is to add a bit of colour. And even that is questionable. They are certainly no deterrent to anyone seeking to gain access to the athletes' quarters. 'Edna Medalia, the former discus thrower who will be my assistant during the race, has no official accreditation, because she isn't included in the delegation, but she walks into the village with no problems using my pass, while Avraham Melamed – who has been excluded from the Israeli swimming team – even stays over in Unit 2, Connollystraße, together with me and four other athletes. He doesn't have a key, so when he came and the door was closed, he jumps in through an open window.' Security at the Olympic Village is anything but airtight. And Black September knows it.

'For me, the first days of the Games follow the usual training routine: I join the Italian group, working with Vittorio Visini, under the eye of Pino Dordoni. Despite the fact that he has no obligations towards me at all, the former Olympic champion treats me as if I were one of his own athletes: he has a passion and a dedication that I had never come across before in all of the European and American coaches I had seen at work. In the time between one session and the next, I go to the Olympiastadion and watch a few races. In the final of the 10,000m, I am left speechless after I watch Lasse Viren fall, get back up, and still win with a world record time. It's the kind of thing you only see once in your life.'

There is one permanent record that Shaul would like to erase. The concentration camp. Much is being made in the media of the fact that the Israeli delegation is competing on German soil. Only 27 years have passed since the US and Soviet soldiers opened the gates of the camps and found themselves staring at mountains of dead bodies and the terrified stares of the survivors. The Eichmann trial is not a historical event – it is recent news. And there are still many former Nazi officers, not as notorious as Eichmann, who are living carefree lives in Germany. These old people, murderers who never faced punishment, are now seeing the Star of David on their TV screens. It is no longer a piece of yellow fabric with the power to decide a person's fate; now the star stands in the middle of a flag that flies among the flags of all nations in Munich's Olympiastadion. In Bavaria. In Germany.

Shaul Ladany is the only survivor of the camps in the Israeli delegation. The others had only heard tales of life inside the *Konzentrationslager* from family and friends. Shaul had lived through it in his own childhood.

'One day, I find the delegation in a frenzy. I discover that there has been a commemoration event at the Dachau concentration camp, around 20 km outside Munich, and almost none of the Israeli delegation – athletes or officials – has taken part. Apparently, this news had reached the Israeli media and provoked a scandal: there are people demanding disciplinary action. I myself receive a very harsh letter from Shosh: she accuses me of not having even the smallest amount of sensitivity, of not being able to pass up a training session even to pay my respects to millions of dead Jews. The simpler explanation is that nobody had told me about this event. Even if I had known, however, I would not have gone. It's not a question of training: nothing to do with my legs, but all about my head and what lies within. I have not yet processed that part of my life. And it will take many more years before I do.'

The mounting controversy in Israel leaves no space for personal preference, however: the delegation officials have organised another ceremony at Dachau in an attempt to calm the waters and smooth over their absence at the previous event. Shaul asks to be excused, on the grounds that he doesn't want to relive certain traumas, but – even though he is the only survivor in the group – he is ordered to attend.

'I walk into the camp, through the gate and the barbed wire, and I stand there by myself, keeping a distance from the others. After the ceremony, they organise a tour of the site, to show us the artefacts and the remains that have been collected. I don't join the tour. I wait outside.'

While this is taking place, the Games are about to crown a young Jewish athlete: Mark Spitz, the swimmer who had stood next to Shaul at the Maccabiah Games. Here in Munich, he has been doing everything he couldn't do in Mexico City: winning every race he competed in, including the relays. And setting a new world record in every one of them. One person winning seven gold medals is an achievement beyond comprehension, so much so that a joke starts to make the rounds of the Olympic Village. 'An athlete meets a colleague and asks him: "Have you heard about Spitz's third place?"

'The other looks at him in shock and asks: "What? He lost a race and only came in third?"

'"No, third place in the nations' medal table."'

Mark Andrew Spitz, a man who stares down at half the world from the heights of the podium. And even more. At the end of the Games, a hypothetical nations' medal table featuring Spitz would have the swimmer not in third place, as in the joke, but in eighth. Unprecedented. Among those he leaves in his wake are Great Britain, which end the Games with four gold medals, five silver and nine bronze.

When he arrives at the starting line for the 50 km racewalk on 3 September 1972, Shaul Ladany is not aiming for a medal. He knows that he is in the best form of his life, however, and is determined to finish higher than at Mexico City.

'I believe I am capable of a time around 4 hours and 10 minutes, which would put me between sixth and twelfth place. Amitzur Shapira comes with me to the stadium and tells me that he will wait there until I return. It's a nice thought, but I need someone to support me around the course . . . luckily, Edna Medalia has agreed to help with my refreshments. It would be convenient to have someone there in the first few kilometres to let me know my pace: I think I have started at a gentle pace, but there is nobody from the Israeli delegation along the road to tell me how much time has passed. When I reach the official timekeeping station at the fifth kilometre, I am in for a good and bad surprise: 23 minutes and 9 seconds. Not only am I going quicker than I had planned, but this is also 30 seconds quicker than my all-time best over 5km. That is a problem, because this event is not a sprint and there are still 45 km to go. I have to slow down, otherwise I risk failing to reach the finish line. I hold back, but at the 10 km mark I am still too fast: 47 minutes and 34 seconds. That's ten seconds under the national record, set by me. The worst moment comes not from looking at my watch, though, but from looking at the personal refreshments table, when I see my Coca-Cola is not there. Where is Edna and my thermos flask with the Coke and glucose? I see her approach the table anxiously after I have already passed it.

'She shouts to me: "Dr Ladany, I'm sorry. I got stuck in traffic."

'I try to continue without losing my confidence, but I know the lack of sugar will have consequences. I drink a bit of water at the next sponging station, but for my own drink I will have to wait for the 15th kilometre, where Edna is already waiting in place. Things continue to go well until the 20 km point: 1 hour and 40 minutes have passed, and I am exactly where I need to be to reach my target time, but I can already feel that I am paying the price for starting too quickly and for the setback at the refreshment point. I'm not the only one struggling: Elliott Denman, who is among the supporters in the crowd, tells me that Pamich, the Italian gold medallist from Tokyo, is out of the race, and later on I overtake the Hungarian, Antal Kiss, who came second in Mexico City four years before. He's looking worse than me. I finish in 19th place, in 4 hours 24 minutes and 38 seconds. It's a good time and a respectable position, but I again regret starting too quickly, not having guidance on the timing, and that missing first refreshment.' The event is once more won by a German, but this time it is the West German, Bernd Kannenberg, who finishes comfortably under four hours (03:56:11), ahead of Soldatenko (USSR, 03:58:24) and Ladany's American friend Larry Young (04:00:46). There are three British athletes in the race, and they all cross the finish line: Paul Nihill, the Tokyo 1964 silver medallist, who comes in ninth (04:14:09), John Warhurst, who finishes in 18th, one place above Ladany (04:23:21), and Howard Timms in 25th (04:34:43).

'The next day, I enjoy something a bit different. In truth, it starts like all the others: even though the race is finished, I head out for a short training session. Then, for the first time since we arrived in Munich, I allow myself a trip into the city to buy a few souvenirs to bring home for Shosh and Danit. In the afternoon

I go back to the stadium and watch a few events: I'll have more time for sightseeing over the next few days. I never imagine that, in just a few hours, every plan will be overturned.'

In the evening, a large group from the delegation decides to leave the village together and head into the city to see a musical. *Fiddler on the Roof* is playing, taken from a book in Yiddish by the author Sholem Aleichem, with Shmuel Rodensky, 'the Israeli Laurence Olivier', in the lead role. 'Our delegation is also invited onto the stage to meet Rodensky, and we take a photo with him. Without the race to worry about any more, I have a wonderful evening, and it is about midnight when we return to Connollystraße, all relaxed and determined to enjoy the rest of our stay in Munich.' Many of the men smiling from that final photo will be dead 24 hours later. An image taken at the airport in Tel Aviv will reunite them, with the survivors standing next to coffins wrapped in the Israeli flag. 'That was the moment I realised just how few of us remained: of the 13 male athletes in the squad, only eight survived.' Despite it being a workday, thousands of people come to the airport to pay their respects to the victims in a ceremony that takes place on the runway. The crowd throng about the survivors, all wanting to touch, embrace and kiss them. They go from Olympic celebration to national grief in the space of a few hours, without the time to process what has happened. For them, the Olympics are over and there are no medals to celebrate. Every delegation coming back from the Games is interested in its returns, but this time it is not podiums and finishing positions which are being counted. There are no winners and losers in the Israeli delegation. Only victims and survivors.

THIRTEEN

WORLD CHAMPION
WITHOUT PERMISSION

The bodyguard has one hand on a pistol, with another weapon strapped to his ankle under his trousers. He has not let Ladany out of his sight from the moment he landed in Switzerland. He lowers himself into an armchair next to the bed. He will spend the whole night there alongside Shaul.

Less than two months has passed since the Munich massacre, and the risk of further attacks remains high. 'I turn down the chance to participate in the London to Brighton, but nothing can stop me from being in Lugano for the "Cento". I knew the risks before the Olympics, and I know them now: I have no intention of stopping. I asked the Israeli Athletics Committee to fund my trip, but the response was negative. After the Games, they are discouraging all athletes from competing abroad: the officials are afraid of being held responsible if there are more victims, so they try to keep us in Israel, waiting for an official security policy to be issued. So, I decide to make my own arrangements.'

Help comes from Hirsch Galitzky, a Swiss jeweller and Orthodox Jew, who has supported Ladany before in his participation in the 100 km event. 'Galitzky is insistent that I participate in the race, so when I tell him that I am not receiving any funding for the travel costs, he offers to pay half. Without the East Germans, who will not be there this year, he thinks I have a good chance of victory.'

That is how Ladany finds himself in Switzerland, flanked by an armed plain-clothed guard and with Hirsch himself, who also carries a pistol. The evening before the race, the three of them travel to Olivone, from where the athletes will depart. They travel in two vehicles, Shaul sitting next to his bodyguard. The booking at the hotel has been made under a false name, and there is an attempt to keep Ladany's name out of the media coverage of the event until the last moment.

The 'Cento' is one of the most important races in the calendar: for an entire week, Lugano becomes the racewalking capital, with competitions of every kind, one day after the next, from relay trials to short distances. The 'Cento' is the climax, the toughest challenge and the most exclusive: there are no world championships beyond the Olympics, not for athletics generally and not for racewalking, but the International Amateur Athletic Federation – the international body – assigns the Swiss event the status of global *criterium*. The course passes through Bellinzona, Locarno on the shores of Lake Maggiore, and then, after 75 km, when the exhaustion really begins to kick in, the athletes climb up the Monte Ceneri pass before descending into Lugano. Not a gentle excursion.

'This time not only am I in shape, but I have also prepared in terms of my diet. After the Olympics, I began to hear talk of a new method of increasing the levels of glycogen in the muscles: in addition to eating more carbohydrates, in the three days before the race I am to eliminate proteins and fats. I tried this diet for a 100 km session in Israel and my body responded excellently, so I decide to try it this time, too. In the evening, before I go to sleep, I fill myself up with pasta, but without sauce. That is the secret: avoiding sauces. It works like a treat: I am able to walk for almost ten hours without problems.'

Galitzky's prediction appears destined to come true. As the kilometres pass, Shaul draws closer to the biggest victory of his career. His Japanese rival Saito is having an off-day, while his friend Badel cannot match his pace despite his best efforts. Ladany sweeps through like a king, his security detail by his side. 'My guardian angels do not let me disappear for a second, not even during the race. I would not give up my shirt with *ISRAEL* written across it for the race. They say that makes me an easy target, but I assume anyone seeing us from a distance will see Galitzky breathing hard as he passes refreshments to me and tells me the distances: my writing might be in block letters, but his black overcoat and hat do not leave much space for doubt about who we are.'

The road from Olivone to Lugano passes with no threat or situations that require the intervention of his bodyguards. Over the last section, Ladany has built up an advantage that is no longer measured in metres, but in kilometres. 'I can enjoy the victory without having to look over my shoulder. As I enter Lugano, I can already hear the loudspeakers announcing my arrival. There are thousands of people waiting for me in Piazza della Riforma, and maybe it's the diet, maybe it's because I'm winning, but this time I am not even tired and I am able to take in everything that is happening around me. The "Cento" is mine.' A triumph that is celebrated in the press, and there is even time for a few moments for Ladany to enjoy his celebrity status, for example when he is brought to a shopping centre in Lugano two days after the race to sign photographs for people.

Back in Israel, however, things go differently for Shaul. Any hopes of a champion's homecoming are immediately crushed: there is no official welcome at the airport. On the contrary. There is a bitter surprise awaiting him at the border, when a police officer recognises Shaul and tells him that he has been referred to a disciplinary committee. He had gone to compete abroad against the wishes of the senior sporting authorities, and now they want to show him who is in charge. Unfortunately for them, their intended prey does not take kindly to attempts at intimidation, and the hearing rapidly deteriorates from inquisition to farce.

'The man responsible for proving the charge is not exactly a genius. This is clear to me from the very beginning, and I am determined to enjoy every minute of this circus. The situation is almost surreal, with my counterpart struggling to make any sense with his questions. "Ladany, you are accused of having travelled without permission. How do you plead?"

"'Not guilty. I don't need permission to travel. I didn't ask for anyone's permission to come here today either."

"'You are accused of having travelled abroad without permission. How do you plead?"

"'Not guilty. Israeli citizens are allowed to travel abroard as they like, so long as they have a valid passport."

'At this point, he starts to rub his forehead, and then I can almost see the relief as he comes up with another question to throw at me: "Do you admit to going abroad for a competition, without permission?"

"'An Israeli citizen does not need permission to travel abroad to compete."

'At this point he doesn't know where to bury himself, so I decide to toy with him a bit, like a cat with a mouse, giving him a few ideas.

"'Try accusing me of participating in the race."

'He comes back to life and resumes the questioning.

"'Do you admit to having competed abroad without permission?"

"'The question is too vague. Reword it."

'This time it is the judge who comes to his rescue.

158

"'You have to accuse him of having participated in a specific race.'

'The man who is supposed to prove my guilt is completely disoriented by this point: he looks through a file in front of him, then another, then finally he comes out with: "Ladany, you know very well which race you took part in."

'I have to hold myself back from laughing in his face.

"'You are the one who has to prove the case against me. Not me."

"'Ladany, tell us which race it was."

'I know I could keep quiet, but then the hearing would only be deferred, and I would have to come back and face the commission again. Better to offer a little more help.

"'Accuse me of having participated in (and won) the international *criterium* 100km race in Lugano, Switzerland."

"'You are accused of having participated in the 100km race without permission. How do you plead?"

"'Not guilty. I have participated in lots of 100 km races: if you want to accuse me, you have to say which race it was, in full."

'It takes him a while to get it right.

"'You are accused of having participated, without permission, at the international *criterium* 100 km race in Lugano, Switzerland. How do you plead?"

'He finishes the sentence with a triumphant smile that lights up his face. It disappears when he hears my response.

"'Not guilty. I admit to participating in that race, but it was not without permission."

'At this point, the judge steps in to take control of the situation.

"'Can you prove it?"

"'And I am more than happy to do so."

'There is an old Arab proverb that says that a man who has been bitten by a snake is also scared of a rope on the ground. In 1965 I had been denied permission to participate in a marathon in Greece, because I didn't have a document from my athletics association confirming my status as a recognised amateur athlete. After that experience, at the start of every year I made sure to ask for such a document to allow me to compete abroad. It was a formality, but one that would be decisive in this case. I had brought those papers with me, and one by one, I pull them out and pass them over to the judge. When I hand over the one from 1972, he turns to my accuser.

"'I would recommend dismissing the case.'"

'My prosecutor has no choice but to do so.'

In the months that follow, Ladany goes to the USA to talk about the Munich massacre on behalf of the Zionist Organization of America: over four weeks, his tour takes him through 20 states, from Massachusetts down to Florida, then west as far as Iowa, Missouri and New Mexico. Shaul goes abroad not only to open his mouth, but also to stretch his legs and return to competing. South Africa offers him the opportunity: the country has been banned from the Olympic Games since 1964 over its apartheid policy, and it is attempting to break its sporting isolation by organising events and inviting leading athletes from around the world.

'Representing Israel with me is the hurdler Esther Shahamorov, another of the survivors from the Munich Games. The South African race policies are clearly a façade – it's enough to see how they treat the black athletes here, who sleep in the same rooms as the white athletes for the duration of the event. At the London to Brighton race, I had made friends with Eddy Michael, who explained what it meant to be a black person under the apartheid regime. He could even crack a few jokes about it and tell me a few stories. Unfortunately, however, it is no laughing matter.'

In his capacity as a professor, Shaul will return to South Africa in 1975 as a guest of the University of Cape Town. During this longer stay – when he wins the South African national 50 km championship – he will come to understand more about the apartheid regime and its hypocrisy. 'I find it interesting how commercial interests overcome anything else. In the early 1960s, South Africa has agreements with Japan worth hundreds of millions of dollars: this causes a problem with Asian businesspeople from Yawata Iron & Steel, who would usually not be allowed into whites-only hotels and restaurants and could not even purchase alcohol without permission. Prime Minister Hendrik Verwoerd's government finds the solution: the Japanese are given the status of "honorary whites". Racial status as an honorific title, rights bartered like goods in the marketplace.

The Japanese are not the only ones to receive such treatment. The title is also afforded to members of New Zealand's All Blacks rugby side when they go on tour to South Africa. For years, New Zealanders with Maori heritage are systematically excluded from tours to South Africa. In 1970, Samoans and Maori are also accepted as 'honorary whites'.

The 1976 tour goes the same way, except the

international situation has become more sensitive in the interim years, and the boycott of South Africa has tightened significantly. One of the protagonists of that tour is Billy Bush, the All Blacks' prop. During the tour, Bush does everything he can to challenge the apartheid system: he brings black girls to the official receptions and introduces them as 'Maori friends from Rotorua'; he goes into the hotel kitchens to talk to the black cooks and waiters; he wanders around the white neighbourhoods after the curfew. The South Africans in turn single him out for special treatment on the pitch, and he finds himself on the wrong side of dubious refereeing decisions. They also pressure the New Zealand officials not to perform the haka, the Maori war dance that the All Blacks perform before every game.

The coach, J.J. Stewart, relays this latter request to Bush, explaining that the South Africans are strongly opposed to allowing a bunch of 'honorary whites' to stick their tongues out at them.

Bush listens. He goes out onto the pitch to play.

And the haka is performed.

FOURTEEN

TO WAR, PAYING HIS OWN WAY

'Are you Shaul Ladany?'

The person welcoming him to the United States at JFK Airport (or, more accurately, welcoming him back) is a customs official. He is also a sports fan, and the water bottle in Shaul's luggage catches his attention. He recognises the owner of the unusual object as the Israeli athlete he has heard so much about.

'Welcome back, Dr Ladany.'

In September 1973, Shaul returns to the USA for a sabbatical: he will be working at Baruch College at City University of New York. 'Shoshana, Danit and I find a place in Riverdale, between Van Cortland Park and the Hudson River, in a flat on the 16th floor with a beautiful view over the Palisades – the cliffs across the river in New Jersey – and the George Washington

Bridge. Over the course of a few days, I fall back into my American life: my workplace has changed, but my racewalking friends are still the same, and the training sessions with John Markon quickly become a Saturday ritual. The first time that we push ourselves too far, ending up on the other side of Tarrytown, I stop at a petrol station to buy a Coca-Cola. The attendant looks at me and comes out with: 'It's been a while since you were here.' I could explain how it's been more than three years since I have walked that road, but I choose a more concise response: 'I'm back.' As we shake off the rust, John and I extend our sessions to over 90km.'

Ladany does not keep himself in shape for the sake of it. At 37 years old, there are no more Olympic goals, partly because the 50km racewalking event has been temporarily removed from the Olympic programme (absent in Montreal 1976, it will return for Moscow 1980). The desire to prove himself with a serious challenge goes beyond the five rings though: for a man who has honed his endurance and stamina, turning them into his most prominent attributes, the drive comes from always raising the bar a little further. At the point where the pain becomes intolerable, Ladany rises above it and finds fulfilment,

It is little surprise then that, when presented with a challenge that many people consider insanity – a test of man's limits that only nine Americans have ever successfully completed – he cannot refuse: 100 miles in under 24 hours.

'The race takes place in Columbia, Missouri, and it is scheduled for the weekend of 5–6 October. The 7th is a holiday, Columbus Day, so I will have time to relax and head back to New York. No rush. In Missouri I meet Larry Young, who is one of only two US athletes ever to have reached the podium at the Olympic Games for racewalking, and the only one to do so twice, after his bronze medal exploits in Mexico City and Munich. Larry is one of the nine Centurions, as those who successfully complete the 100 miles in under 24 hours are known. This time, however, he will limit himself to a few dozen miles: he is not training much because he has taken up sculpting and is moving to Italy soon for a few years.'

Four hundred laps of the track. That is the horizon which is constantly around the corner for the 40 participants competing in the 100 miles, all ready to go round in circles like hamsters on a wheel, a form of self-inflicted torture. No pain, no gain. And, over 100 miles, there is plenty of pain.

The challenge Shaul is about to face is different to anything he has done before: a race of this length calls for more than a few sugary drinks with extra glucose; the body needs solid foods, as the hunger eats away at your stomach and then drains your muscles. And that is before you take into account the outside temperature, which can cause shivers as the sweat freezes on your skin while walking through the night.

'I prepare a bag full of spare kits, while for the next 24 hours my meals will be slices of bread and jam, and sandwiches filled with salted boiled potatoes. That is all I need.'

For the first three hours, everything goes according to plan: from the start, Ladany lets his more imprudent rivals steam ahead for a while, before pushing into a commanding lead as each of them attempts to pass the time as best as they can: some form into small groups and chat as they go, and some have brought small pocket radios and listen to music.

'At one point, as I move to lap him, John Markon tells me about something he heard on the radio of another of the competitors: it appears that fighting has broken out in Israel, but the news didn't give too many details. I try to find out more when, half an hour later, I pass another participant with a pocket radio, but he hasn't heard anything. I have no choice but to catch up with the holder of the first radio: another hour passes until I draw level with him, but he is unable to tell me much more. The same is true an hour later when I lap him once more. In my head, I am trying to come up with a plausible scenario: is it only border skirmishes, blown out of proportion by a local American radio station, or something more serious? Only a week ago, the Israeli Air Force had taken down six Syrian fighter planes . . . I slow down and walk alongside the person with the radio, waiting for the next news broadcast, but the station continues to play music, so I go back to my regular pace. In the meantime, I continue to think: if a war has broken out without warning, it must have happened during Yom Kippur, the holiest day in the Jewish calendar, when even TV and radio stations go dark, and it becomes far more difficult for the army to mobilise the reserves. If that is what has happened, Israel is in serious danger. I have to confirm my fears: I stop next to one of the judges and ask him to place a reverse charge call to Shosh. Two hours pass before the call comes back, but there is no news. In fact, there is no news at all, because it seems I had given him the wrong number. We had only moved to Riverdale a few weeks earlier, and I am struggling to remember the number by heart. I ask him to try again and ask for the right number from the information service. He comes back an hour later, and this time he has a message from Shosh. 'It's all under control. Keep going!' That helps me to relax, and I focus on the race once more.

As the sun sets, it begins to rain, and the track, which is made of cinder and not rubber, quickly floods. The first and second lanes are under almost 10 cm of water, and in order to walk I have to move to the outside, to the third lane, increasing the distance I have to cover. The mud makes things worse: I am covered in it, and my shoes get progressively heavier, not to mention that it has also got inside and is destroying my feet. When it finally stops raining, many hours later, I try to improve the situation by cleaning myself with a bucket of water and changing clothes. That helps, even though when I take my socks off, I see that my feet are covered in blisters and some of them are filled with blood. And that is ignoring the fact that, 75 miles in, there is not a single muscle that doesn't hurt. In those moments you understand the true meaning of an old racewalking expression: the strength of those who cover long distances does not lie in their legs, but in their teeth. They have to be strong for when you grind and grit them in moments such as this. The only thought in my head is to finish it as soon as possible, and when I am down to the last four miles, I even find the strength to pick up the pace a bit. Larry Young joins me for the last four laps and pushes me on. After 399 laps I feel like I'm flying, and I complete the last 400 m to the finish line in 1 minute and 52 seconds. After 19 hours and 38 minutes, I can finally rest. I am the tenth man in the United States to racewalk 100 miles consecutively in under a day.'

Shaul finishes the race exhausted and devoid of energy, too tired to stay and celebrate his success. Despite his original plans, he decides to go back to New York straight away. Barely standing, he takes the bus to St Louis. A few hours later, on the plane back to La Guardia, he reads the *New York Times* and discovers that the fighting in Israel is more than serious, it is critical: the Yom Kippur War has broken out.

Israel had underestimated the intelligence that arrived from different quarters and had allowed itself to be taken by surprise by a coordinated attack from Egypt and Syria. For months, war had been considered imminent yet improbable. Up until a few days before the conflict broke out, there were those within the Israeli military who were pushing for preventive action.

On 4 October, two days before they were attacked, General Israel Tal asked chief of staff David Elazar to reinforce the borders and mobilise the reserves. 'If I am wrong and you are right,' said Tal, remembered in Israel as the creator of the Merkava tank, 'we will have disrupted the holiday plans of the reservists and wasted money. But if I am right and you are wrong, we will be facing a potential disaster.'

The warnings of Tal and other Cassandras like him go unheeded. Warnings from King Hussein of Jordan have no impact, and, as during the Six Day War, the United States' attention is turned elsewhere, with President Richard Nixon caught up in the middle of the Watergate scandal. Israel decides on a partial mobilisation of reserve soldiers on 5 October, more or less at the same time as Ladany is starting his 100-mile racewalk in distant Missouri. Egyptian troop movements near the Suez Canal and the news that the Soviets have recalled the families of their diplomats in Syria are further signs that cannot be fully ignored.

A delayed and partial mobilisation can offer only a limited response, however, when Egyptian troops begin to cross the Suez Canal on 6 October, with air support from 200 fighter planes and a barrage from 2,000 cannons pointed at the Bar-Lev Line. At the same time, the Syrians penetrate into the Golan Heights. Israel is caught in a pincer.

'As soon as I get home, hobbling, I call the Israeli embassy in Washington from the airport, to try and understand just how bad the situation is. They pass me on to the military attaché, and when I introduce myself as an officer in the Artillery, he asks me when I last served. It has been only six months.

'"If you are willing to fly to Israel at your own expense," he replies, "we will find you a seat on the first flight that leaves tonight." I tell him that I already have an open ticket, without a date on it.

'Shosh tries to convince me not to go. "The army doesn't need you," she argues, "and you hate being called up even for drills and periods of high alert. You just want to feel important. Do you not remember how after the Six Day War you said they would have won it even without you?"

'She's right in what she says. She doesn't want to relive the anxiety and stress of the Six Day War and the Munich massacre, that took place just over a year ago. But I cannot stay: I would never forgive myself. It goes beyond a sense of duty.'

Shaul leaves not because he has to, but because he cannot do otherwise. Being so far away would not be a sufficient excuse; it would be merely an alibi, a way to soothe his conscience. The United States is a safe haven, and over the years, it would not be difficult for Shaul to apply for a green card and for them to settle down there. But that option is never on the table for him and Shoshana. And their shared reason is the same reason why Ladany is ready to return to war: 'Israel is our homeland.' At 10 p.m., he and Shosh are saying their goodbyes at JFK.

'There are more than 400 of us boarding the El Al jumbo jet. Unlike six years ago, this time Israelis living abroad flood back to help.

'The flight takes off in the middle of the night, and even though I have been awake for almost 48 hours, I cannot sleep. There is a lot of commotion on the plane, people coming and going along the aisles constantly looking for friends and comrades from their units. I am mostly writhing in pain with every movement. Every so often, the direct flight is interrupted with updates that come in from over the speakers: during those moments everyone goes completely silent. When we are about to land, we are instructed to switch off all the lights and pull down the window-blinds. Outside, below us, Tel Aviv is completely dark to minimise the risk of attack. We land in darkness.'

It is Tuesday evening, 8 October 1973, the third day of the war. Israel attempts to launch its first counterattack, to no avail.

The balance of power is overwhelmingly stacked against Israel, in terms of troop numbers as well as equipment and technology. Egypt and Syria are backed by the entire Arab world: Jordan, Iraq, Algeria, Libya, Morocco, Saudi Arabia, Tunisia, Lebanon and Sudan provide soldiers, weapons and financial support that, taken together, amount to three times more than Israel can put up. In Israel, serious consideration is being given to the nuclear option. At the same time, international diplomatic efforts are taking place to prevent such an escalation, and the United States promises Israel enough weapons to compensate for its losses.

'It is after 8 p.m. when I call the liaison office of my unit. I am told that the regiment has been positioned in the same area as two months ago and I should reach them as soon as possible. The problem is that there is no public transport: I have to get a lift to an undefined location in the Jordan Valley, somewhere near Sartaba. What should I do? I call my sister Marta and ask her to come and pick me up.'

Having paid for his ticket from New York to Tel Aviv, Ladany now improvises the rest of his journey to war. Some of the way by car with Marta, then another stretch with an officer he met on the flight, then hitchhiking the rest of the way.

'I find myself in Jerusalem, on a dark street somewhere near the Lion's Gate. There is no light coming from anywhere and the silence is absolute. It takes an hour before a military vehicle picks me up. From there I hitch another two rides, one as far as Jericho and the other from there to Gilgal. We arrive in the middle of the night. It's 1.30 a.m. and I'm fully alert, waiting for a missile attack that is expected at 2 a.m.. While I wait, I get in touch with the regiment commander, who asks me to go straight to my battery. It has been deployed approximately 15 km from Gilgal, and he clearly thinks I am going there on foot. 'Ladany, you're a racewalker,' he says. 'I'm sure it will be no problem for someone with your training.' He has no idea that I have been awake for almost three days, that my feet are full of blisters and that I am barely able to stand. In my state, with my equipment on my back, 15km feels like madness. I walk along the road, waiting for a vehicle to pass. Luckily, the Jordanian bombardment doesn't arrive, and after an hour, a lorry passes by. The driver takes me all the way to the guard post of my battery, and I am incredibly grateful to him: not only for saving me the exhaustion, but also for sparing me from having my body filled with bullets. Seeing a dark shape advancing through the darkness, the guard would almost certainly have opened fire first and asked me to identify myself later. This way, I am here, safe and sound. Seventy hours ago, I was in Missouri, preparing for the most intense race of my life. Now I am in a war zone, a metre away from the Jordanian border, and the only thing I want is to sleep. I pass out on a nearby rock, with my backpack for a pillow.'

The area is relatively quiet: Jordan is on the side of Syria and Egypt but does not seem to want to open a third front. The reports coming in from Sinai, on the other hand, are of enormous casualties. Ladany engages in a discussion with his sergeant, Shmuel Miller – one father to another – on the pain of losing a child in war, Shaul takes the view that the pain is worse for a family with only one child, while Shmuel – who is older and has a son and a daughter – says there is no difference. The next day, Miller is summoned for a conversation with the regiment commander, where he finds out that his son, a lieutenant in the paratroops, is among the fallen in the Battle of the Chinese Farm, one of the bloodiest exchanges in the Yom Kippur War.

The commander of the 143rd Armour Division in that battle is Ariel Sharon. Among the commanders serving beneath him is a 31-year-old lieutenant colonel whose career as a young officer has intertwined with Shaul Ladany's recent past. Only a few months previously, in April of the same year, he had carried out Operation Spring of Youth: disguised as a woman, he guided an elite commando team who infiltrated Beirut via the coast and killed three senior members of the PLO (Muhammad Youssef Al-Najjar, Kamal Adwan and Kamal Nasser) who were believed to be responsible for the Munich massacre. His name is Ehud Barak, and in 1999–2001 he will serve as prime minister of Israel. His successor in the role would be his commander in that battle, Ariel Sharon.

On the active fronts, in just over two weeks, the tables have turned; the Israelis have crossed the Suez Canal and cut off the Egyptian 3rd Army, coming within 100km of Cairo. Over on the Syrian front, Damascus is closer still. On 22 October, following pressure from the United States and the Soviet Union, a ceasefire is called. There are over 2,500 fallen soldiers on the Israeli side, and over 15,000 on the side of Egypt, Syria and the other Arab nations.

However, the end of the fighting does not mean Shaul is free to return home. 'For three weeks I have not been able to speak to Shosh. Every so often the soldiers in my unit travel to the nearby village of Argaman, and from there they use a public telephone to call their families. The commander of the regiment has promised me that he will find a way for me to call the United States, and apparently the communications officer has taken the assignment seriously. He works for hours before finally giving me the signal. I find myself in a trench underneath a canvas that is partly for protection, partly for camouflage. It's 2 o'clock at night. I pick up the receiver of the field telephone and speak with the regiment operator. He passes me on to the battalion operator. Then on to the regional command operator. Then central command. Then to the general staff. Every single operator along the chain has been told about my call to the United States. One of them, before transferring the signal, tells me that he was a former student of mine. From the general staff, the call is delivered to the civilian operator responsible for intercontinental calls. Within the space of a minute, the telephone is ringing, and then I hear Shosh's voice.

'I cannot believe it: I'm in the middle of nowhere, next to a bulky field telephone that is sitting inside a leather satchel and doesn't even have a disc to dial the numbers, only a receiver. And I'm speaking with my wife in New York.

'I'm so overwhelmed that I don't even notice that I'm raising my voice: the next day I discover that I had woken up all my companions, who heard every word I said. The only bad luck is that Danit is already asleep, so I cannot talk to her.'

No harm done. *Aba* is on his way home. Safe and sound once more.

FIFTEEN

HAPPY BIRTHDAY, DR LADANY

When you are a 37-year-old athlete, there is always somebody there to remind you that you are old. It doesn't matter that you have only just begun to truly enjoy yourself, it changes nothing that only now have you truly understood how to live. For too many people, the only thing that matters is the date on your birth certificate. Which is only ever a relative parameter: at the university, anyone below 40 is a young professor with their whole life ahead of them. Anything but old. But the day always arrives when you are asked if your career as an athlete is over. And you have no specific moment in mind. You have no idea how to respond, for the simple reason that you never stopped feeling like an athlete. That is what happens to Shaul Ladany: the years pass, but he keeps marching on, only his objectives change. There are no more call-ups to prepare for, but the desire is still there. More podiums, more prizes: the overlapping voices of the announcers and the trips that become a pleasant distraction from an intensive academic career full of lessons, exams and research.

The passion for racewalking, however, is not universally shared by his seniors at Tel Aviv University. 'One day, the Dean tells me that I have to make a decision: sport or academia? I tell him that I made my decision a long time ago: I prefer the sport, but I commit fully to my academic obligations. In five years of teaching at Tel Aviv, I have published 14 articles in scientific journals, registered four patents in the USA, edited two dictionaries of statistics terminology, and sent to press another ten studies for trade magazines. Obviously, that must have been a hobby to fill all that spare time I had between training sessions and competitions.'

In 1975, Ladany transfers to Ben-Gurion University. It is there, in Be'er Sheva, that he builds the rest of his career. From that city, swallowed up in the Negev Desert, Ladany continues to travel abroad to teach from time to time. Cape Town, Berlin and Singapore are just a few of his destinations. But more often than not, his destination is the United States, and to Atlanta more than anywhere else, returning on several occasions to Emory University and Georgia Tech. Atlanta is the city of Coca-Cola, and will later be chosen to host the Olympic Games. A celebration for Shaul, who still has many friends in the area. A tragedy when, on 27 July 1996 – in the middle of the Olympics – a bomb goes off in Centennial Olympic Park during a concert with thousands of people. The bomb leaves two people dead and 111 injured, and thoughts immediately return to Munich 1972. This time, however, it is not an act of international terrorism. No Black September. The culprit is a US citizen, Eric Robert Rudolph, not yet 30 years old, an extremist anti-government radical who decides that his preferred form of protest is to place a bomb underneath a park bench.

A few days after the Atlanta bombing, Shaul begins training again as a full athlete, and signs himself up for the Israeli 50 km national racewalking championship. At the age of 60, the national title is once more his. For the 28th time. Shaul Ladany and racewalking in Israel are one and the same. An icon.

In the meantime, the Ladanys have made their home in Omer, a small city on the outskirts of Be'er

Sheva. Shaul's house is easy to identify, even for those who don't know him personally. A cursory glance is enough. On the wall is an outline in wrought iron, a design so simple that it could have come from the pen of Osvaldo Cavandoli himself. It's not his famous character, 'The Line', however, but a stylised racewalker wearing glasses. 'When we move into this neighbourhood, there are not many houses: our garden faces onto the desert, and animals often cross into it in search of food. That's no problem as long as it's frogs and porcupines, but one time Danit calls me, scared and screaming: there's a snake that has decided to make its home at the back of ours.'

The desert gradually gets further away, replaced by new neighbours. The dangers are not all nature-related, however: every so often, the siren system goes off, warning residents to go into the bomb shelters. Less than 50km stand between this peaceful residential area and the Gaza Strip – the distance of a race for Shaul Ladany which becomes a trail taking a few short minutes for Grad missiles. Explosions from one side and incursions from the other: when the alarm goes off, the war enters people's homes, and it is better not to stray too far from a safe area. Despite everything, Omer remains the centre of the

Ladany family's life, the home they return to after every sabbatical and every race.

During the summer months, Shaul still enjoys travelling to Europe. 'I enjoy the long, non-competitive events. One I particularly like is the Paris to Tubize – around 300 km in four days, finishing outside Brussels. I also try never to miss the Haervejsmarch in Viborg, in Denmark, and the Vierdaagse in Nijmegen, in the Netherlands.'

In 2002, Shaul is ready to go back on the road. His tickets are booked, and he is looking forward to wearing himself out alongside his old friends, chatting to them in three or four different languages. Shoshana is the one who first notices the swelling on his thigh, near his groin: it's nothing too large, and more importantly, it doesn't hurt. Shaul is persuaded to go and get himself examined by a doctor: after all, what if it causes discomfort during an event?

The doctor asks a few questions, takes a look at his legs, then orders a series of tests, one of them a biopsy. It's not an injury; it's a lymphoma. Cancer. 'It takes me a while to grasp the situation: I ask the doctor if I can still go to Europe – I have already arranged everything. He tells me that I have to begin chemotherapy and radiotherapy. I understand.'

The lymphoma is in the early stages; it is important to tackle it as soon as possible. The side-effects of the chemotherapy are rough: coming home from a round of treatment leaves Shaul exhausted, struggling to eat, wanting to move and unable to do so.

'It is only after several days, when the next treatment is already around the corner, that I can walk around the house a bit: I roll up the carpets, open the doors and create a small home circuit of 20–30m for myself. Doing laps makes me feel better. I feel alive.

'After the third round of chemotherapy, the signs are encouraging: the disease has regressed. At this stage, the protocol demands a fourth round, but I do not agree. I don't want to feel ill for the sake of it. The tests say that things are better, and there is no sense continuing just to tick the boxes. I argue this point with my doctor, who does not want to take the responsibility for my stopping the treatment. I ask the opinion of two haematologists. The lymphoma has been in regression for a while and I have a physique that means my body responds differently to those of most people my age, partly thanks to my training. I can stop the chemo. I am recovered.'

Shaul celebrates in his own way: three months after the diagnosis, he takes part in a short-distance racewalk. Another three months go by, and he starts the new year by completing a marathon. A return to racewalking is a return to life, one step at a time. Pushing the barrier a bit further each time used to be a metaphor for finding new limits for his body. Now, increasing the distance is a way to quantify the extent of his recovery: one metre gained is one doubt defeated. And every new medal is not only a prize, but also recognition of the tenacity with which he fought the disease. Not even the lymphoma can bring a halt to a tradition that Shaul has upheld since 1962: the Sea of Galilee Swim. Over 4 km in the water, which feels like a recovery test for Ladany. If he can overcome that, he is ready for anything. 'In recent years I have taken part in the race without training, and the last time I have swum was in last year's race. And in all honestly, I don't even enjoy swimming that much: I learned to swim after we were released from Bergen-Belsen, when we were in Switzerland. One day my mother took me to the river, the Rhine, and in a single afternoon she taught me to swim.' An effective lesson if Shaul can continue to plunge into the water without fear some 60 years later. The Sea of Galilee Swim is an annual fixture, however, while walking remains a daily pleasure, made even more special by several extraordinary achievements that Shaul refuses to turn down, for example in 2006.

One more mile makes a hundred. One more year and he will turn 71. So much time has passed since the last time Ladany covered a hundred miles that he has taken the decision to try again. 'The pain passes after a week, but the satisfaction of reaching the finishing line stays with you for the rest of your life.' It is a common refrain among marathon runners. Words that appear to be carved into Shaul's legs. The date is 18 May 2006, and Ladany is determined to inflict this athletic martyrdom on himself once more: his lifelong friend Ron Laird – veteran of four Olympic Games with Team USA – has organised everything in his home town, Ashtabula in Ohio, an hour away from Cleveland by car. Some 20,000 inhabitants follow the efforts of this Israeli who has been training by Lake Erie for the past month. Over 21 hours 45 minutes and 34 seconds, Ladany completes laps of Smith Field, proving that 70 years are not too many.

Hundreds of laps that resemble a giant circle coming to a close: as an academic, Ladany is reaching the end of his last sabbatical year before returning to Israel to conclude a teaching career spanning over four decades and to take on the title of professor emeritus. Shaul's walk is one of reconciliation, sliding the pieces of his life into place, one after the other.

'After he left Germany, my father-in-law, Ludwig Ahlfeld, swore to himself that he would never again set foot on German soil. One day he was flying somewhere on behalf of the United Nations – he was an architect and town planner – when his plane landed in Germany for a technical stop: all the passengers left the plane, while he insisted on remaining on board. He could not break his vow. I see it differently. I don't feel any resentment towards the Germans; they admitted their guilt, and as far as I'm concerned that is a vital step, because it means accepting what took place and taking the responsibility for it. Since that first, traumatic visit to Dachau in 1972, I have visited other concentration camps. Together with Shosh, I even went back to Bergen-Belsen, and began to look for materials and images. In 1995, on the 50th anniversary of the liberation of the camp, I organised an exhibition at the university of the things I had found and collected. I still have very clear memories in my head, vivid images and feelings of the hours spent standing in the cold while the Nazis counted us again and again, shouting. I still remember the face of one of the guards . . . me and the other kids, we called him Popeye, because he reminded us of the cartoon character. I remember it well, but I sleep well at night: I have no nightmares, nobody chases me through my dreams.'

Shaul keeps marching forwards and looking ahead, but he doesn't forget. He even refreshes his memories occasionally, even the more recent ones. 'I went back to Connollystraße. I was in Munich for work, and I decided to go back to the building, which has since become more famous than the stadium which hosted the Games. I asked for directions from a lady, who replied to me very politely in German. After a while, I arrived at the door and rang the bell of the accommodation where I had stayed during the Games. To my surprise, the same woman who had given me directions opened the door, but when I explained to her who I was and asked if I could see my former room, she did not react well. Nervous. I'll never understand that.'

Sometimes there is nothing to understand, all you can do is move on. And not even retirement can stop Shaul, who starts every day with 15km before he goes to his office on the campus. First floor, room number 169: here Professor Ladany continues to receive researchers and collaborators. After 13 books, over 100 publications and 8 registered patents, his body of work has been celebrated with a lifetime achievement award for his contribution to engineering management. A prize that he proudly displays alongside the one from the IOC, the Pierre de Coubertin medal for his contribution to the Olympic movement.

The plaques are tributes to hang on the wall, but walking is an ongoing celebration which starts up anew every time he sets off. Age is not a problem for Shaul, merely one more variable to factor into the equation. 'As time goes by, every kilometre feels a little longer, every mountain a little higher, and every climb a little steeper, but I'm not worried. I believe it's normal.'

It started from the idea that every kilometre adds something to life. And that the reverse is also true: that every day contributes to making the road ahead that bit more interesting. From there, Shaul adopted a method of celebrating his birthdays, from the 50th onwards. Wherever he finds himself, he walks 1km for every year of his life. He even completed it in the humid heat of Singapore, because such a tradition does not allow for exceptions. On occasion he even got it wrong, such as on his 71st birthday, when he accidentally walked 75km. But Shaul Ladany has always been one for rounding up. One kilometre more extends your life. And for once, there is no rush to reach the finish.

SIXTEEN

SURVIVING IS UP TO CHANCE, LIVING AGAIN IS A CHOICE

The two of us are the only ones on the road. Me and him. He is Shaul Ladany, the survivor.

'Dr Ladany, I suppose,' I greet him, in the 5 a.m. darkness of a deserted Jerusalem street.

How does one recognise a man who survived the Holocaust?

How does a boy who lived through Bergen-Belsen age?

What is left of the athlete who walked for thousands of kilometres only to come within a few steps of death?

What clues do two wars leave on the face of a soldier?

The answer to all these questions is standing there in front of me, in a tracksuit, impatient to start walking.

I meet Shaul Ladany by the starting line of the

Jerusalem Marathon: the race is not due to start for another two hours, but he has received permission from the organisers to set off early, so that he can finish before the time limit at racewalking pace.

Two minutes after we introduce ourselves, our legs and arms are in motion.

The story can start.

Interviewing a racewalker while walking alongside them is like interviewing a boxer while serving as their sparring partner. Albeit less painful. In the worst case, you will end up with sore legs at the end.

Shaul Ladany talks as he goes, and the tale stretches out into an infinite sequence of steps.

That first meeting was followed by others at his house, in his office and along the streets that he made his own by marching along them time and again. In addition to the fatigue, we also shared meals, books and the occasional discussion. While picking over a falafel, I discovered that Shaul has been a vegetarian since the age of 5. Watching him at work, I noticed how his life has seeped into his work: he uses the Hebrew alphabet when he writes, but not when he types. With a keyboard in front of him, he feels more comfortable with the Roman alphabet, and leaves it to his assistant to copy his notes.

I have seen him with his family and asked his oldest granddaughter, Shaked, what she thinks about having a grandfather who insists on waking up at dawn to spend hours walking. She thinks about it for a moment, and says, 'None of my friends have a grandfather like him.'

Danit – Shaul and Shoshana's daughter – grew up between Israel and the United States with a father who was different to the others, a father who was always on the move. She traces his perpetual motion back to a single word: willpower.

It is the strength of character that pushes Shaul. You can survive only to die from within. Or you can push beyond it. Shaul Ladany did. Several times. He transformed his endurance into an existence marked and measured in kilometres. He did not crumple under the pain: he stored it up and unspooled it like a ball of yarn along the road. It is perhaps no coincidence that, as an athlete, he was drawn to racewalking: one foot in front of the other, always moving forwards, never turning around. The further you go, the stronger your endurance. And every step carries you further away from what you left behind.

You can put thousands of kilometres beneath your feet, but certain experiences cannot be washed away with the sweat. They are always there, your shadow on the road. Distorted and terrifying, but on the move.

A reminder that you are alive.

AFTERWORD

THE FIRST STEP

On Professor Ladany's 80th birthday, I walked alongside him, participating in that ritual of movement through which he marks the passing of time: 80 kilometres for 80 years. The more ground we covered, the closer we became.

Years passed before I was comfortable calling him Shaul, as opposed to Professor Ladany. Even in training shorts and a vest, he remains the emeritus professor from Ben-Gurion University. He continues to stretch his legs every day, but never at the expense of his research: committing his studies to paper or to the whiteboard before confirming them on the screen, column upon column of numbers reflected back through the thick lenses of his glasses. Every so often, I wonder whether our relationship is actually two separate ones: do I walk alongside Shaul and speak with the professor? A few minutes in his company are enough to realise that there is no such distinction. With Shaul Ladany, it is all one and the same.

And over those 80 kilometres of walking together, we found the right space.

That day felt like the outline of another chapter being written into the asphalt of the roads around his house. The sun was yet to rise over the Negev Desert when we set off, and we kept walking until just before the dusk that marked the onset of the Sabbath. Thirteen hours spent side by side. Professor Ladany delivered his latest lecture, while Shaul shared his fatigue, countless stories and reflections.

I recall one in particular, seemingly a purely sporting anecdote. 'I have dedicated myself to racewalking for almost 60 years,' he told me. 'I have walked my way through every stage of life, but if I think a bit deeper about the way in which I have faced it, perhaps I should consider myself a hurdler more than a racewalker. In those challenges, where the space from the start to the finish is filled with row after row of hurdles, you cannot permit yourself to stop and think about the hurdle you have just overcome.

You don't stop if you hit one of the hurdles, even if it knocks you off balance and makes you stumble.

'The hurdles behind you are gone, for better or worse. The only thing that matters is the next hurdle, the one in front of you.'

I had never thought of him as a hurdler, but thinking about it, I cannot help but agree: he is a hurdler of life.

He survived the Holocaust, fought in wars in the Middle East, came through a terrorist attack, overcame cancer, and then – after all of that – he lost his lifetime companion. Shoshana Ladany passed away on 14 September 2018. 'We were married for almost 58 years and never argued – not once,' the professor wrote to me, when he informed me of his wife's passing. In his final years by her side, Shaul had to face yet another enemy, one with the power to make memories vanish and push even the closest faces out of recognition. Shosh's Alzheimer's diagnosis was a painful sentence, and a daily struggle to live with, but it was nothing compared to the pain of coming to terms with her absence in the days that followed, after having shared a lifetime with her.

'I am still in love with Shosh and her memory,' says Shaul. 'I did not have the mental strength, nor the will, to remove her clothes and other belongings from our wardrobes, cupboards and drawers, or even from the coat hangers by the door. Occasionally, when I visit flea markets and I see a pepper mill she didn't have, I buy it and add it to Shosh's collection, which is still on display on the shelves in our kitchen.'

A man afflicted by some of the most traumatic events of our age may appear outwardly unshakeable, he may seem as if he has lost his sensitivity. That is not the case. Here too, in the face of a grief so deep and so personal, Professor Ladany's approach remains the same. It is an ode to life.

He does not suppress the past. On the contrary, he is a man who nurtures his memory in every form. The thousands of collections that leap out from every corner of his house – from stamps to simple household objects – are proof of that. Shaul does not forget. He remembers everything: people, places, moments and sounds. A piano sits in his living room, one of the few items the Ladany family was able to recover from their house in Belgrade. A piano that Shaul's mother was deeply attached to, and which children, grandchildren and great-grandchildren have all played – with varying degrees of success. Those keys – those notes – have travelled from 1930s Europe to the present-day Middle East. And as painful as the memories might be, they have never held Shaul back from living, from finding a new tune within.

Although few of us will ever live through the scale of global tragedies that he has survived, we all have times when we are forced to deal with personal and often overwhelming pain.

The road Shaul Ladany has walked is more than a simple overview of 20th-century history. It is a story that offers us direction and purpose in the face of obstacles in our own lives.

However severe and insurmountable they may seem at first, there is only one way to tackle them: taking the first step.